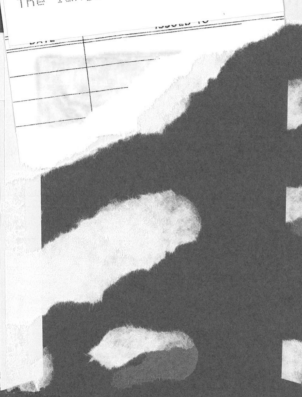

The Language(s) of Poetry

The Language(s) of Poetry

WALT WHITMAN, EMILY DICKINSON, GERARD MANLEY HOPKINS

James Olney

GEORGIA SOUTHERN UNIVERSITY

JACK N. AND ADDIE D. AVERITT

LECTURE SERIES

NO. 2

24322

The University of Georgia Press

Athens and London

© 1993 by the University of Georgia Press
Athens, Georgia 30602
All rights reserved
Designed by Betty Palmer McDaniel
Set in 10/14 Janson Text by Tseng Information System, Inc.
Printed and bound by Thomson-Shore, Inc.
The paper in this book meets the guidelines for permanence
and durability of the Committee on Production Guidelines
for Book Longevity of the Council on Library Resources.

Printed in the United States of America

97 96 95 94 93   C   5 4 3 2 1

Library of Congress Cataloging in Publication Data
Olney, James.
The language(s) of poetry :
Walt Whitman, Emily Dickinson,
Gerard Manley Hopkins / James Olney.
p.   cm.
"Jack N. and Addie D. Averitt lecture series."
Includes bibliographical references and index.
ISBN 0–8203–1485–4 (alk. paper)
1. American poetry— 19th century—History and criticism.
2. Whitman, Walt, 1819–1892 — Criticism and
interpretation.   3. Dickinson, Emily, 1830–1886 —
Criticism and interpretation.   4. Hopkins, Gerard Manley,
1844–1889 — Criticism and interpretation.
I. Title.   II. Title: Language of poetry.
III. Title: Languages of poetry.
PS316.O43   1993
811'.309 — dc20   92–12564
CIP

British Library Cataloging in Publication Data available

For Laura

Contents

Foreword

James Olney, Voorhies Professor of English and French & Italian at Louisiana State University and coeditor of the *Southern Review*, delivered *The Language(s) of Poetry: Walt Whitman, Emily Dickinson, Gerard Manley Hopkins* as a set of three lectures at Georgia Southern University on October 7 and 8, 1991. The lectures were the second in the annual series of Averitt Lectures, which alternate year by year between the Department of History and the Department of English and Philosophy. The first set of lectures, by Eugene D. Genovese, was published as *The Slaveholders' Dilemma: Freedom and Progress in Southern Conservative Thought, 1820–1860* by the University of South Carolina Press in 1992. Professor Olney's lectures seek to discover what unites and distinguishes the poetry of Whitman, Dickinson, and Hopkins and to investigate the common grounds of modern poetry, for whom these three poets are "precursors." If it seems that Professor Olney could scarcely have chosen three more eccentrically different, or opposed, poets, both in personal demeanor and poetic technique and subject, that choice nonetheless drives irresistibly toward a satisfying inevitability. It is difficult to convey the sense of excitement at the time of those in the audience who were witnessing this process. And always the discussion of the "poetics" of these authors was fresh, informed by a critical acumen that did not exclude the personal ("I" is not absent from these lectures). The lectures fulfilled the goals of Jack N. and Addie D. Averitt when they provided for them: Professor Olney's lectures have enhanced the quality of the professional and academic life of the university, and they have advanced significantly the scholarship of an important field of inquiry.

Acknowledgments are due to R. Frank Saunders, Jr., who, as chairman of the joint English-History Averitt Lectures Committee, time and again gave our department's Averitt Lectures Committee valuable assistance and advice; to James R. Nichols, head, Department of English and Philosophy, and Walter J. Fraser, Jr., head, Department of History, for their strong encouragement and support; to Mrs. Esther Mallard of the History Department whose help in planning the social activities was indispensable to their success. I want especially to thank my fellow committee members for their enormous contributions in time, energy, and eclectic expertise throughout the entire process, from its first planning stages through its completion in this book: these valued associates are Professors David L. Dudley, Patricia Ingle Gillis, Richard Allen Keithley, Patricia Ann LaCerva, Dale Purvis, and Frederick K. Sanders. Finally, on behalf of the committee, the departments of English & Philosophy and History, and Georgia Southern University, I want to express our appreciation to the Averitts, whose foresight and generosity made these lectures possible in the first place.

All of us on the Averitt Lectures Committee are pleased and proud to have been a part of the process that has resulted in *The Language(s) of Poetry: Walt Whitman, Emily Dickinson, Gerard Manley Hopkins*. These chapters are more elaborately developed than the original lectures could be, given the constraints of time and the lecture format. Professor Olney has presented his poets in ways that provide fresh insights into the "languages" of their poetry and that we believe make an enduring contribution to the study of poetics.

John B. Humma, *Chairman*
English and Philosophy Averitt Lectures Committee

Preface

The invitation to deliver the Jack N. and Addie D. Averitt Lectures for 1991 was a most welcome one and came for me, as I now look back on the occasion, at a particularly propitious time. Had the invitation come either earlier or later I am sure that it would have been equally welcome, but I suspect that in such a case I would have chosen to address a different subject and would no doubt have conceived of the project in quite a different manner than I have done in the present book. As it was, the invitation arrived when I was engaged in directing a graduate seminar on modern poetry in the English department at Louisiana State University. I had chosen to focus the work of the seminar on three "precursors" of modern poetry—Walt Whitman, Emily Dickinson, and Gerard Manley Hopkins—who, I argued, could be seen to have been profoundly determinative of the shape and the nature of modern poetry in English. With this work already in hand— and it seemed to me that, largely through the agency of a wonderful group of graduate students, the work became constantly more exciting and alluring as we discovered new riches in the reading of poetry virtually every day of the term—it was altogether natural to continue, in one form or another, with the same subject and with the same three poets for the Averitt Lectures. Indeed there was a pleasing symmetry about the program of three poets and the format of three lectures—not that I ever intended to set one lecture for each poet, for this would not have served my purposes at all, but what I wanted to say about the language(s) of poetry seemed to me nicely sayable in three parts—three lectures in the first instance, three chapters now—on three poets as different from one another but as open to speculative comparison and alignment/realignment as Whitman, Dickinson, and Hopkins.

The lectures, though they were churning around in my mind during the last couple of months of the modern poetry seminar, were written only after the semester was over—in fact, several months after it was completed, when I could recollect in tranquillity the thought, and perhaps some of the emotion as well, of the seminar. A direct consequence of the work of the seminar, the lectures were nevertheless designed from the outset not as a kind of report on the seminar but as something that would answer to the terms of the Averitt Lecture series as described in the program notes: "Jack N. and Addie D. Averitt established this lecture series as a gift to the Departments of History and English and Philosophy at Georgia Southern University. The purpose of the lectureship is to enhance on-campus academic and cultural life for students, faculty, and community." This, I thought, set forth a noble purpose for the lectures, and it suggested doing something not of a highly specialized nature that would appeal to a select few but something rather that might speak to those outside as well as inside the university and to an audience from right across the disciplinary spectrum. I had this in mind as I wrote the lectures, and I can only hope that what I have produced in some way corresponds to the intention—both to my own intention and to the intention of the Averitts in their generous sponsorship of this lecture series. The lectures were written pretty much as they appear now as chapters in this book; presented as lectures, however, they were of necessity considerably briefer than the present text. I remember well the psychological pain I suffered in striking out passage after passage from the original manuscript to reduce it to manageable lecturing form; but I also remember well the consolation that I kept offering myself with the assurance that these excluded passages could all be restored when it came time for publication. And that has now been done. Thus is assuaged the hurt done to a cut and slashed manuscript—or, it may be, the hurt done to an author's vanity.

Although I have changed much in going from lecturing to publishing, mostly by way of restoring an original text, I have not attempted to remove from the printed version all traces that would suggest a speaking occasion. The separate chapters here were intended, in their inception and completion, as lectures for reading, and that sense of them was—and is—so strongly with me that I want to encourage the silent reader to imagine them always as being read and heard viva voce, especially so the passages of poetry, which constitute, and very deliberately on my part, an extraordinarily large proportion of the text. Indeed, if I were to make a suggestion about how best to read this book, it would be to read aloud the passages of poetry, particularly those in the first chapter. I like to think that the reading of the poems in the course of presentation gave the lectures whatever distinctive quality they may have had, and it would please me to think that readers could on their own avail themselves of the distinctiveness conferred on the lectures by the voices of Walt Whitman, Emily Dickinson, and Gerard Manley Hopkins.

There are a number of people I must thank for the parts they played in the making, the delivery, and the publication of these lectures. The first is David Dudley who telephoned the original invitation to me, then arranged all details of my visit to Georgia Southern University with care and efficiency, and finally, with his wife Eileen, saw to my comfort and happiness throughout the time I spent in Statesboro. Others who acted the part of generous hosts at Georgia Southern, and who looked to my welfare both physical and spiritual while I was in Statesboro, were Professor John B. Humma, chairman of the Averitt Lectures Committee for 1991; Dr. James R. Nichols, head of the department of English and Philosophy; Gautam and Bela Kundu, former colleagues at LSU and now at Georgia Southern, who hosted a splendid dinner party; and Eric Nelson, who, himself a fine poet, offered some particularly cogent comments and questions on the lectures. Dean Emeritus Jack N. Averitt and Mrs. Addie D. Averitt not only made these lectures possible through their generous bequest but they were also present to add luster as well as insight to the occasion of the lectures. To these old and new friends at Georgia Southern University I am deeply grateful, as I am also to those people at the University of Georgia Press who have done everything to make the transformation of the Averitt lectures into a book as easy for the author as it could possibly be: Malcolm L. Call, the director of the press and a friend of long-standing; Matt Brook, as thoughtful an editor as any author could wish for; and Michael D. Senecal, who has proved an ideal copyeditor. At LSU Michael Griffith has given expert assistance in proofreading and indexing, and conversations with Dave Smith, my colleague at the *Southern Review*, helped me in thinking through all the issues of *The Language(s) of Poetry*. Finally, three people read all parts of the manuscript of this book—and some parts more than once—and gave me advice and suggestions that have resulted in an immeasurably improved book: Susan Morehouse, who, aided by her two-year-old daughter Lora, provided me with pages of extremely helpful notes; Donna M. Perreault, who took time from preparing an excellent dissertation to bring me back several times to the right track in pursuing my argument; and, most of all, Laura O'Connor, who not only assisted me greatly with matters both of content and style in the actual writing of the lectures but who also helped me plan and think through the seminar on which the lectures were based.

The Language(s) of Poetry

CHAPTER ONE

Sprung Rhythm,
Common Meter,
and the Barbaric Yawp

In a well-known passage in the preface to the *Lyrical Ballads*, Wordsworth wrote, "They who have been accustomed to the gaudiness and inane phraseology of many modern writers, if they persist in reading this book to its conclusion, will no doubt frequently have to struggle with feelings of strangeness and awkwardness: they will look round for poetry, and will be induced to inquire by what species of courtesy these attempts can be permitted to assume that title." There is a certain irony, of course, in the fact that after the poetic revolution effected in large part by these same *Lyrical Ballads*, the situation changed to the degree that if something claiming to be a poem did *not* sound like the *Lyrical Ballads*, then readers looked round for poetry and not finding what they expected denied these attempts the title of poetry. Every age has, no doubt, its sense of what is and what is not poetry (and parenthetically I should remark that the poets of any age are always in advance of the age itself — in advance of the consensus of the times — with respect to what is and what is not poetry). When Matthew Arnold declares of Dryden and Pope that "[t]hough they may write in verse, though they may in a certain sense be masters of the art of versification, Dryden and Pope are not classics of our poetry, they are classics of our prose," one is left to imagine what either Dryden or Pope would have said of Arnold's own "Dover

Beach" or his "Philomela"; and what would any of the three—
Dryden, Pope, or Arnold—have had to say of Walt Whitman[1] or
Emily Dickinson, of Sylvia Plath or Allen Ginsberg, of Langs-
ton Hughes or Amiri Baraka? Would they, by some species of
courtesy, have permitted the attempts of these writers to assume
the title of poetry? Or in the reverse perspective, would Baraka
or Plath or Whitman grant the title of poetry to the writings of
Arnold, Pope, and Dryden? The sense of what is poetry in any
given age is, at least in large part, historically and culturally determined, and I think this will be readily enough granted; but that is
not here my subject. Rather than a historical survey of what has
been thought to be poetry, or the language of poetry, in different
ages, I want instead to try to discover if there are any elements
of language usage in poetry that are constant from century to
century or cultural context to cultural context. Now, the poets I
will give primary consideration to are all poets of the past 100 or
125 years; and what I take poetry to be is certainly, inescapably
conditioned by my own historical and cultural circumstances, my
historical and cultural limitations if you like. Nevertheless, I think
it is possible to say something about the language(s) of poetry that
will be not entirely hostage to the historical, cultural moment of
its saying; but it is necessary to maintain a delicate balance here,
for the poets I will be giving close consideration to were unquestionably products of their times, even though in certain ways they
might stand apart from those times, and an appropriate reading of
their poetry must situate itself at that point where the language of
the time, the nearly ahistorical language of poetry, and the unique
way with language of this particular poet all converge to produce
the felt meaning of a specific text.

From the time in 1983 that I took up duties as coeditor and
sometimes sole editor of the *Southern Review* until today, I have
been faced with the task of reading (by a conservative estimate)
some four or five thousand pieces of writing a year that presented
themselves as poems to be considered for publication in the jour-

nal. In 1990, which I should think was a reasonably representative year, we published from among those four or five thousand submissions only 121 poems, so the question of what it was in those 121 poems that made them seem to be poetry of a higher order than the forty-five hundred rejected items is a matter of some real importance for me. I'm sure that there are all sorts of intuitive and unconscious things going on in making these editorial choices, but I believe that at least some general points can be made that would indicate, in a rough and ready way, why these 121 poems and not 121 totally different ones were chosen. Another recent experience has contributed also to my choice of subject for these lectures and to many of the illustrative examples I will be giving for what I want to say. A year ago I was put down to direct a graduate seminar in modern poetry and chose to concentrate the term's work on three poets whom I took to be "precursors" of modern poetry: Walt Whitman, Emily Dickinson, and Gerard Manley Hopkins. Leaving Hopkins aside for a moment, I can imagine a reader particularly devoted to Dickinson who, coming to Whitman, "will look round for poetry, and will be induced to inquire by what species of courtesy these attempts can be permitted to assume that title," and likewise for the devotee of Whitman who takes up Dickinson's writing.[2] I chose not to divide the semester's work into three parts with a section given over to each of the three poets but rather to mix them together so that, after the first few weeks, we had readings from each of the three poets for every seminar meeting, and thus the radical differences that separate Whitman's from Dickinson's poetry were before us constantly and were the very substance of the seminar. I can testify, as could everyone else in the seminar, that to go from Whitman to Dickinson (or vice versa, as we had no set order for taking them up on any given day) produced the effect of a very severe psychic wrenching. I will go into this matter more fully a bit later but will leave it here with the observation that it was sometimes difficult to keep in mind that it could be said equally and alike of Whitman and Dickinson that (in the words of a Dickinson poem) "[t]his was a poet."[3] If one of them, it sometimes seemed, then not the other, and if the other, then not this one. But obviously this only makes the problem more urgent and more acute, for at this late date neither Whitman nor Dickinson can be denied their greatness as poets; so what is it in their language—languages I would say—that makes them undeniably poets, and great poets at that?

There are, I will argue, three properties to the language use of Whitman, Dickinson, and Hopkins, or of any writer whom we take to be a poet, that would cause us to feel that what they write is what we understand by "poetry." These are: a heightened rhythmization of language; a heightened figurativity of language; and a personal use of the language, a personal formation or deformation of the language, to an extraordinary degree—what I will term "making strange" with the language. I would not claim that there is anything radically new in the observation that the language of poetry is always characterized by heightened rhythmization, heightened figurativity, and a kind of eccentricity of usage, but I do believe that we may come to understand the nature of poetry more clearly and more surely by examining these properties in three poets as widely different among themselves as Whitman, Dickinson, and Hopkins. I should also point out that my three headings are not neatly distinct one from another but rather overlap and occur at all points in any poem to make the poet this particular poet and none other; nevertheless, I am going to focus on each of the three separately in three separate lectures as if they were not all of them entangled and inseparable—with, however, some time at the conclusion of the final lecture given to an attempt to see these three elements as integral aspects of the poet's singular achievement.

To begin, then, with the heightened rhythmization of language: Rhythm is one of those words (like the word "time" in St. Augustine's description of it in the *Confessions*) that we use frequently and familiarly and whose meaning we know very well—until we are asked what it might be; then we are lost. Perhaps the problem is that we use the word vaguely and in too many different senses, and when we want to use it in a reasonably specific way these other senses hover and distract us from the task in hand. What I shall mean by "rhythm" is the more or less ordered recurrence of units of sound, which, in their recurrence, establish the pattern or design of a poem. As I will be referring to meter and metrical verse, let me say that I take meter to be a special instance of rhythm; it is rhythm regularized and demonstrable (in English poetry) by measuring and counting—measuring the stress placed on different syllables and counting the number of syllables in a line. (Parenthetically, I should observe that no quasi-scientific field of inquiry is as confused and as confusing as the study of prosody. Prosodists seem temperamentally given to self-assurance and certainty in their analyses of lines of verse, but you will scarcely find two prosodists who will agree about any single line.) In the three poets who provide our primary illustrations of the rhythmization of language we have a very wide rhythmic-metrical range, from the hymnodic metrical regularity of Emily Dickinson in many of her poems to the highly rhythmic but entirely nonmetrical poetry of Walt Whitman, with Gerard Manley Hopkins occupying a middle ground of poetry that is markedly rhythmic in various ways and even metrical, but not according to any traditional or inherited system of metrics. Dickinson adopted and adapted the traditional meters of English hymns, while Whitman and Hopkins created their own unique rhythmic forms; all three were rhythmic revolutionaries, unique in their time but powerful and pervasive influences in the poetry of the century that followed their achievements.

I have been speaking as if rhythm were a matter only of lines of verse and of whole poems, but while it is true that this is where rhythm may be realized and localized I think it is equally true that we can speak of a poet's characteristic rhythm or rhythms and mean by that, at least speculatively, that there are bodily and

mental rhythms specific to this poet that are reflected or are mani-
fest in the rhythms of the poetry. Think of Emily Dickinson and
you think in terms of certain kinds of movement, both physical
and verse movement; think of Walt Whitman and you think in
terms of certain very different kinds of movement. And I believe
it is not mere insignificant linguistic coincidence when we speak
of the "body" of a poet's work, or of a poem "embodying" figuratively those same rhythms that the poet literally "embodies" and
shows forth in the typical stance and movement of the body. Paul
Valéry, the French poet who probably gave more sustained attention to the nature of the creative act than any other writer of the
twentieth century, implies in the discussion of the genesis of certain of his poems that the rhythm of a poem can be, on the one
hand, something altogether prior to the words, the imagery, or the
subject matter of the poem and, on the other hand, the apparent
consequence of physical movement and bodily posture or stance.
Valéry tells of having gone for a walk one day "to relax from some
tedious piece of work" and, he says, "As I went along the street
where I live, I was suddenly *gripped* [Valéry's italics] by a rhythm
which took possession of me and soon gave me the impression of
some force outside myself." His "movements in walking," according to Valéry, "became in my consciousness a very subtle system
of rhythms."[4] As human gaits differ, one must suppose that the
rhythms that came to possess Valéry were specific to his gait and
would be quite different for a poet with a different gait. This, at
any rate, is what Seamus Heaney suggests in an interesting essay
on the characteristic movement in the poetry of Wordsworth.
After quoting Hazlitt, who wrote that both Coleridge and Wordsworth composed their poetry while walking in the open air—but
with this difference: that Coleridge "liked to compose in walking
over uneven ground, or breaking through the straggling branches
of a copse wood; whereas Wordsworth always wrote (if he could)
walking up and down a straight gravel walk, or in some spot where
the continuity of his verse met with no collateral interruption"—

Heaney picks up on Hazlitt's remark that, in reading, "Coleridge's manner is more full, animated and varied; Wordsworth's more equable, sustained and internal," and continues thus:

> Wordsworth's chaunt acted as a spell upon the hearer, whether that hearer were Hazlitt or Wordsworth himself. It *en*chanted. It was "equable, sustained, internal," three adjectives which we might apply to the motion of Wordsworth's blank verse also. The continuity of the thing was what was important, the onward inward pouring out, up and down the gravel path, the crunch and scuffle of the gravel working like a metre or a metronome under the rhythms of the ongoing chaunt, those "trances of thought and mountings of the mind" somehow aided by the automatic, monotonous turns and returns of the walk, the length of the path acting like the length of the line. And I imagine that the swing of the poet's body contributed as well to the sway of the voice, for Hazlitt tells us that "there was something of a roll, a lounge in his gait, not unlike his own Peter Bell."[5]

What Heaney, following Hazlitt, implies, as also does Valéry, is that there are bodily rhythms, perhaps mental rhythms as well, common to all of us—best suggested, perhaps, by the systole and diastole of the heartbeat, that pulse and impulse coincident with life itself—that cause us to desire and even require analogous rhythms in our means of expression; beyond this, however, Heaney, Hazlitt, and Valéry seem agreed that there are not only these rhythms common to us all, but that there are in addition rhythms peculiar to the individual poet, to Wordsworth, Coleridge, or Valéry, reflected alike in the poet's physical carriage and in the voice that composes and performs the poem.

I will take up in a moment the special and specific rhythms that we might think of as Whitmanian, Dickinsonian, and Hopkinsian, but I want to return briefly to Paul Valéry and what he has to say about rhythm and the making of certain of his poems.

I stress "certain of his poems" because the poetic process begins in different ways with different poems.

> Sometimes it is the will to expression that starts the game, a need to translate what one feels; another time, on the contrary, it is an element of form, the outline of an expression which seeks its origin, seeks a meaning within the space of my mind. . . . Note this possible duality in ways of getting started: either something wants to express itself, or some means of expression wants to be used.
>
> My poem *Le Cimetière marin* began in me by a rhythm, that of a French line . . . of ten syllables, divided into four and six. I had as yet no idea with which to fill out this form. Gradually a few hovering words settled in it, little by little determining the subject, and my labor (a very long labor) was before me. Another poem, *La Pythie*, first appeared as an eight-syllable line whose sound came of its own accord. But this line implied a sentence, of which it was part, and this sentence, if it existed, implied many other sentences. (*The Art of Poetry*, p. 80)

T. S. Eliot testifies in a similar vein to this rhythm-before-idea genesis of his own poetry when he writes, in an essay titled "The Music of Poetry," "[A] poem, or a passage of a poem, may tend to realize itself first as a particular rhythm before it reaches expression in words, and . . . this rhythm may bring to birth the idea and the image."[6] Thus rhythm comes, or may come, before word, image, or idea, and it also goes beyond the very words out of which it composes itself—or so Eliot implies in another passage in the same essay where he claims that meaning, rhythmically or musically created, continues to exist at a level to which the dictionary sense of words cannot attain. "If, as we are aware, only a part of the meaning [of a poem] can be conveyed by paraphrase," Eliot writes, "that is because the poet is occupied with frontiers of consciousness beyond which words fail, though meanings still exist" ("The Music of Poetry," pp. 22–23). There are poems by Hopkins, by Dickinson, by Whitman that we can explain and explicate all day and yet come away with the feeling that there is a meaning, a deeper meaning, that we have not touched at all, a meaning that can be realized only by a reading, by a performance in which the rhythm is allowed to exercise full sway. This is why, as I have long felt, the analysis of a poem in the classroom in terms of diction, imagery, theme, and so on should always be concluded with a reading that gives itself over entirely to the felt rhythms of the poem.

I have already alluded to the psychic wrenching that occurred in our Whitman-Dickinson-Hopkins seminar when we moved from Whitman to Dickinson or Dickinson to Whitman. This recurrent minor trauma was largely, if not entirely, a consequence of the radically different rhythms of the two; it was as if the seminar had been possessed of a single nervous system that, having become attuned and accustomed to the expansive, rhetorical, repetitive, frequently incantatory and hypnotic rhythms of Whitman could not, at least not without considerable effort and readjustment, move into the angular, ironic, contained and compressed metrical regularities (which, however, admit many irregularities) of Emily Dickinson. There are all sorts of reasons why it should be difficult, or near impossible, to move from a characteristic (some would say bombastic) passage in "Song of Myself" to a poem like #449 of Dickinson, but surely the most important reason is the mind set or the neurological disposition/predisposition established by the rhythms of Whitman's poem, which make us anticipate an indefinite continuation of his swelling, engulfing lines—only to be brought up short and sharp by the so-called Common Meter of "I died for Beauty." (I would say, parenthetically, that it is very difficult to choose brief passages from Whitman for illustrative purposes: it is precisely his engulfing onward flow and expansiveness that is so characteristic of Whitman, and once one starts to read it is virtually impossible to find the right place to stop. *Leaves*

of Grass is one long poem that ended only with Whitman's death;
it did not, however, conclude even then, for there truly is no conclusion in Whitman. The way to read Whitman is to read him
at length. Dickinson, by contrast, wrote in units of individual,
discrete poems, and the way to read her is to concentrate all of
one's powers of understanding on the word, the line, the stanza,
and the single poem—but hardly beyond. The *wrong* way to read
her, as I discovered when I attempted it as a graduate student, is
to read right through the 1,775 poems from the first page to the
last of Thomas Johnson's standard edition, *The Complete Poems of
Emily Dickinson.* There is no more astonishing poet in the English
language than Emily Dickinson but as readers our capacity to be
astonished is not limitless, and if we simply read straight through
the *Poems* we will finally, through sheer loss of energy, fail to reg-
ister or respond to that sharp edge of brilliance and originality
that is Dickinson's signature effect.) I will look more closely at the
rhythmic properties of these and other passages later but here are
some lines from Whitman and one complete poem from Dickinson that I take to be altogether characteristic of the two of them
rhythmically:

Walt Whitman, a kosmos, of Manhattan the son,
Turbulent, fleshy, sensual, eating, drinking and breeding,
No sentimentalist, no stander above men and women or apart
    from them,
No more modest than immodest.

Unscrew the locks from the doors!
Unscrew the doors themselves from their jambs!

Whoever degrades another degrades me,
And whatever is done or said returns at last to me.

Through me the afflatus surging and surging, through me the
    current and index.

I speak the pass-word primeval, I give the sign of democracy,
By God! I will accept nothing which all cannot have their
    counterpart of on the same terms.

Through me many long dumb voices,
Voices of the interminable generations of prisoners and slaves,
Voices of the diseas'd and despairing and of thieves and dwarfs,
Voices of cycles of preparation and accretion,
And of the threads that connect the stars, and of wombs and of
    the father-stuff,
And of the rights of them the others are down upon,
Of the deform'd, trivial, flat, foolish, despised,
Fog in the air, beetles rolling balls of dung.

Through me forbidden voices,
Voices of sexes and lusts, voices veil'd and I remove the veil,
Voices indecent by me clarified and transfigur'd.

I do not press my fingers across my mouth,
I keep as delicate around the bowels as around the head and
    heart,
Copulation is no more rank to me than death is.

I believe in the flesh and the appetites,
Seeing, hearing, feeling, are miracles, and each part and tag of
    me is a miracle.

Divine am I inside and out, and I make holy whatever I touch or
    am touch'd from,
The scent of these arm-pits aroma finer than prayer,
This head more than churches, bibles, and all the creeds.

If I worship one thing more than another it shall be the spread
    of my own body, or any part of it,
Translucent mould of me it shall be you!
Shaded ledges and rests it shall be you!

Firm masculine colter it shall be you!
Whatever goes to the tilth of me it shall be you!
You my rich blood! your milky stream pale strippings of my life!
Breast that presses against other breasts it shall be you!
My brain it shall be your occult convolutions!
Root of wash'd sweet-flag! timorous pond-snipe! nest of
    guarded duplicate eggs! it shall be you!
Mix'd tussled hay of head, beard, brawn, it shall be you!
Trickling sap of maple, fibre of manly wheat, it shall be you!
Sun so generous it shall be you!
Vapors lighting and shading my face it shall be you!
You sweaty brooks and dews it shall be you!
Winds whose soft-tickling genitals rub against me it shall
    be you!
Hands I have taken, face I have kiss'd, mortal I have ever
    touch'd, it shall be you.

I dote on myself, there is that lot of me and all so luscious,
Each moment and whatever happens thrills me with joy. . . .
                              ("Song of Myself," section 24)

> I died for Beauty—but was scarce
> Adjusted in the Tomb
> When One who died for Truth, was lain
> In an adjoining Room—
>
> He questioned softly "Why I failed"?
> "For Beauty", I replied—
> "And I—for Truth—Themself are One—
> We Brethren, are", He said—
>
> And so, as Kinsmen, met a Night—
> We talked between the Rooms—
> Until the Moss had reached our lips—
> And covered up—our names—
>   ("I died for Beauty," #449)

I hope the reader can sense the psychic cost involved in moving directly from section 24 of "Song of Myself" into the Dickinson poem. Adapting Dr. Johnson on the metaphysical poets, one could fairly say that the most heterogeneous rhythms have been yoked by violence together. I do not claim that I have the schizophrenic reading right, but I must acknowledge that I practiced going from Whitman to Dickinson without a break and a restorative breath-taking many times before hazarding it here. Thank God for Hopkins, as I had occasion to feel more than once during the course of our modern poetry seminar—Hopkins who, sharing something with Whitman and something with Dickinson, kept the psyche of the seminar more or less together. Here is Hopkins in "Binsey Poplars," a poem of almost pure sound lamenting the felling of a row of aspens along the River Isis just outside Oxford:

> My aspens dear, whose airy cages quelled,
> Quelled or quenched in leaves the leaping sun,
>> All felled, felled, are all felled;
>> Of a fresh and following folded rank
>>> Not spared, not one
>>> That dandled a sandalled
>> Shadow that swam or sank
> On meadow and river and wind-wandering weed-winding bank.

> O if we but knew what we do
>> When we delve or hew—
> Hack and rack the growing green!
>> Since country is so tender
> To touch, her being so slender,
> That, like this sleek and seeing ball
> But a prick will make no eye at all,
> Where we, even where we mean
>> To mend her we end her,
>> When we hew or delve:
> After-comers cannot guess the beauty been.

> Ten or twelve, only ten or twelve
> Strokes of havoc unselve
> The sweet especial scene,
> Rural scene, a rural scene,
> Sweet especial rural scene.

With these three widely different but obviously rhythmic passages echoing in our minds — each, as I believe, characteristic of its author — I would like to consider some of the rhythmic properties and rhythmic effects of these and other poems. I have been insisting that poetry displays a *"heightened* rhythmization" of language, rather than simply claiming that it is a rhythmic ordering of language, because I want to distinguish the rhythms of poetry from those of prose — for prose, too, has its appropriate rhythms, less obvious, less insistent perhaps, less amenable to metrical analysis, but rhythms all the same, the rhythms proper to prose. There are certain rhythms governing my speech even as I talk to you now, rhythms determined by the slowness or rapidity of my talking, by the pauses in my speech, and by the emphases placed more on some syllables and words than on others; were the lecturer someone other than myself the rhythms of his or her speech would doubtless be quite different from mine. An instance of prose that is without doubt rhythmically organized came to my attention a few years ago when I was reading Gertrude Stein's book *Everybody's Autobiography*. Describing a trip to the United States during which she expected to go from Chicago to Iowa City but was prevented by a snowstorm, Stein writes, "and you never can tell and we did not get to Iowa City. I would like to have seen Iowa. Carl and Cook come from Iowa, you are brilliant and subtle if you come from Iowa and really strange and you live as you live and you are always very well taken care of if you come from Iowa."[7] As I come from Iowa myself, I was very taken by this passage, and so I engaged a free-lance designer to letter the passage in a form that I could hang on my office wall. The designer did a very interesting and, I think, intelligent thing: She evidently read the passage over and conceived of it as something very much akin to eight lines of free verse à la Walt Whitman and displaying rhythms that would not be out of place in Whitman's poetry. She did not turn it into full-blown free verse by starting each line with a capital letter, but she did lay the lines out as Hopkins (if not Whitman) might have done to indicate the number of syllables and/or stresses in each line. Would this not do as a passage of free verse?

> And you never can tell
> And we did not get to Iowa City.
> I would like to have seen Iowa.
> Carl and Cook come from Iowa,
> You are brilliant and subtle if you come from Iowa
> And really strange and you live as you live
> And you are always very well taken care of
> If you come from Iowa.

Or this, with the lines laid out as in the lettered wall hanging and with punctuation added in the manner of Whitman, who virtually never had run-on lines (I believe that Stein imagined that her rhythmic units were so strong that they would be capable of replacing the punctuation that Whitman used to mark the unit ends):

> . . . and you never can tell,
> And we did not get to Iowa City.
> I would like to have seen Iowa.
> Carl and Cook come from Iowa,
> You are brilliant and subtle if you come from Iowa,
> And really strange and you live as you live,
> And you are always very well taken care of,
> If you come from Iowa.

I do not claim that this is a very great poem, except perhaps in its sentiments, which to my ear have a certain grandeur about them, but it does seem to me to demonstrate that the rhythms of prose, especially Gertrude Stein's prose, are not far removed from the rhythms of some kinds of poetry. As Stein was writing prose, she did not, as my designer did, break her sentences into verse lines, but I believe nevertheless that her ear heard the passage in rhythmic units—units that could well have been lines— even as she composed it in her own patented kind of sentences. If this is so, then, in this passage at least, Stein was as much a writer of poetry as of prose, for in poetry, unlike prose, the line is an essential rhythmic unit—indeed I would say that today (and this may always be true) the line is *the* essential rhythmic unit. The line in prose is arbitrary and insignificant—a result of the way the printer sets the piece up in type—but in poetry, and particularly in free verse since there are normally no other rhythmic units than the line, it is crucially determinative. (In fact, I would say that much of the free verse being written today, where it is unsuccessful is so because, just as with prose set up in type, the line is arbitrary and insignificant. I am tempted to reproduce here lines from a poem submitted to the *Southern Review* that shows little or no sense of the integrity of the poetic line, the consequence of which is that if one attempts to observe line ends in reading the piece there is a loss of prose sense without any corresponding gain in rhythmic sense. But I must trust that the reader will see that this is what would happen without being offered proof since professional ethics do not permit the use of such material.) I make these remarks about the rhythms of poetry and the rhythms of prose because I want to look more closely at Whitman's poetry, which has been accused of being nothing but prose—and very prosaic prose at that—chopped up into lines of varying lengths.

The strongest, the funniest, and the most perverse case against Whitman's poetry was made by the twenty-two-year-old Henry James reviewing *Drum Taps* in the *Nation* in 1865. "It has been a melancholy task to read this book," James begins, "and it is a still more melancholy one to write about it." After scolding and lecturing Whitman at some length on his subject matter, James takes up the question of his form:

> Mr. Whitman's primary purpose is to celebrate the great-
> ness of our armies; his secondary purpose is to celebrate the
> greatness of the city of New York. He pursues these ob-
> jects through a hundred pages of matter which remind us
> irresistibly of the story of the college professor who, on a
> venturesome youth's bringing him a theme done in blank
> verse, reminded him that it was not customary in writing
> prose to begin each line with a capital. The frequent capitals
> are the only marks of verse in Mr. Whitman's writing. . . .
> [E]ach line starts off by itself, in resolute independence of its
> companions, without a visible goal. But if Mr. Whitman does
> not write verse, he does not write ordinary prose. . . . Our
> author's novelty . . . is not in his words, but in the form of his
> writing. As we have said, it begins for all the world like verse
> and turns out to be arrant prose. . . . But what if, in form,
> it *is* prose? it may be asked. Very good poetry has come out
> of prose before this. To this we would reply that it must first
> have gone into it. Prose, in order to be good poetry, must
> first be good prose.[8]

James, for all his youthful self-confidence, could hardly have been more wrong, as he later recognized and acknowledged,[9] but it is easier to say this—that James was wrong in his early assessment of Whitman—than to demonstrate just exactly how Whitman's poetry escapes being what James termed it: "arrant prose." The dual key to any demonstration that Whitman was writing not arrant prose but poetry of a very high order must come, I am con- vinced, first, in the perception that the line is the rhythmical unit for Whitman—and he was a very great master of the line—and, second, that his poetry has close ties to oratory or public rhetoric and so reveals its inner nature most fully in performance. With

Whitman, more than with almost any other poet (although Hopkins more than once makes this claim, and justifiably I believe,
about his own poetry), the greatness is to be felt in the reading—
I mean actual reading aloud, chanting or singing or crooning
or whatever the verse demands—or it will not be felt at all. My
own appreciation of Whitman, I have to admit, was rather late
in coming. I suppose I agreed early on with the person, whoever
it was, who said, "Whitman was the greatest American poet of
the nineteenth century—alas!" But then I remember the moment
when, to a freshman English class struggling with E. M. Forster's
A Passage to India, I decided to read from the source of Forster's
title, Whitman's "Passage to India." I do not believe that "Passage
to India" is Whitman's finest poem—"Song of Myself," "Crossing Brooklyn Ferry," "Out of the Cradle Endlessly Rocking," "As
I Ebb'd with the Ocean of Life," "When Lilacs Last in the Door-
yard Bloom'd," and "I Sing the Body Electric," as well as some
of the shorter poems from "Children of Adam," "Calamus," and
"Drum Taps" are all, in their various ways, stronger and more im-
pressive achievements than "Passage to India"—but I must confess
to a particular fondness for the latter poem, for it was in reading
it aloud to my freshman class that I was suddenly convinced, not
by argument but by rhythmic possession, of Whitman's greatness
as a poet.

Singing my days,
Singing the great achievements of the present,
Singing the strong light works of engineers,
Our modern wonders, (the antique ponderous Seven outvied,)
In the Old World the east the Suez canal,
The New by its mighty railroad spann'd,
The seas inlaid with eloquent gentle wires;
Yet first to sound, and ever sound, the cry with thee O soul,
The Past! the Past! the Past!

. . . .

Passage O soul to India!
Eclaircise the myths Asiatic, the primitive fables.

. . . .

Passage to India!
Lo, soul, seest thou not God's purpose from the first?
The earth to be spann'd, connected by network,
The races, neighbors, to marry and be given in marriage,
The oceans to be cross'd, the distant brought near,
The lands to be welded together.
A worship new I sing,
You captains, voyagers, explorers, yours,
You engineers, you architects, machinists, yours,
You, not for trade or transportation only,
But in God's name, and for thy sake O soul.

What can be said of Whitman's rhythms, their power and their
particularity? I think there are two useful sources for gaining some
sense of Whitman's rhythms, both as a man and as a poet, one
of them most unlikely, the other as likely as the first is unlikely.
The unlikely source is T. S. Eliot, as recorded by Donald Gallup,
talking on the subject of "Walt Whitman and Modern Poetry" to
members of the Allied forces in London during World War II; the
likely source is Whitman himself in the three anonymous, highly
laudatory reviews that he wrote of the first edition of *Leaves of
Grass*. I call Eliot an unlikely source, first, because he was not
known to have written or talked about Whitman at any length
until we published Gallup's account of Eliot's 1944 talk in the special number of the *Southern Review* devoted to Eliot in 1985; and,
second, because as far back as 1917 Eliot had declared that there
was no such thing as *vers libre* or free verse, and anyone committed
to that position would not seem to be the most probable source
of enlightenment about Whitman's poetic practice. What Eliot
wrote in 1917 was that "the ghost of some simple metre should
lurk behind the arras in even the 'freest' verse; to advance men-
acingly as we doze, and withdraw as we rouse. . . . [F]reedom is

only truly freedom when it appears against the background of an artificial limitation. . . . There is no escape from metre; there is only mastery." [10] By 1944 Eliot was willing to recognize exceptions to his earlier strictures with regard to free verse and meter—or maybe I should say that he was willing to recognize *an* exception. "There are two kinds of free verse," Gallup has Eliot saying; but then, perhaps recalling his earlier claim that "*vers libre* does not exist," he immediately qualifies with the rider "or rather two things which pass under that name," and then he continues thus: "one, verse in which regular and established meters are broken up almost—not quite—out of recognition. The pleasure one gets out of the irregularity of such verse is due to the shadow or suggestion of regular meter behind. Another kind of free verse—rarer and more difficult (in fact, hardly possible, unless one is born to it)—is the verse which has a particular rhythm for that author, with no suggestion of a familiar meter behind it. Whitman's is of this type." Whitman, according to Eliot, was the reverse of a "traditional" poet, whether one means by that term the poet who starts a tradition or one who follows what was started by others. As both man and poet, Whitman had an overwhelmingly powerful personality, reflected in a "purely personal rhythm," the consequence of which is that "you cannot imitate Whitman. . . . Whitman is better than he appears on first acquaintance; at first reading, his poems seem to go on and on. When you study and reread them, you find that they cannot be compressed or shortened without mutilation; nor can Whitman's verse be made more rhythmical as poetry. It is perfect, although at first it looks far from it. This singularity is very great and makes Whitman unique in the whole history of literature." [11] This, of course, does not define Whitman's rhythms or his rhythmic particularity since the singular and the unique cannot be defined, but what Eliot says does help us to see that there may be poetry, and of the highest order, that is such largely if not entirely on rhythmic grounds.

When, in his three self-reviews, Whitman describes himself, his posture, his stance, his gait, and so on, we are made to recall the comments of Heaney and Hazlitt with regard to the lived, living rhythms of Wordsworth and Coleridge, but there is a difference in that Wordsworth and Coleridge blended personal rhythms with received metrical forms while Whitman claimed only personal rhythms (or, if not only personal, then personal and national) with no suggestion of received metrical forms. "An American bard at last!" Whitman exclaims of his own book and of himself. "One of the roughs, large, proud, affectionate, eating, drinking, and breeding, his costume manly and free, his face sunburnt and bearded, his postures strong and erect. . . ." [12] The reviewer Walt Whitman could be sure that this dawdling, swaggering movement, at ease and comfortable in the body, was the internal and external rhythm proper to *Leaves of Grass*, for the poet Walt Whitman had told him so in "Song of Myself": "I loafe and invite my soul, / I lean and loafe at my ease observing a spear of summer grass"; and near the end of the poem, "I too am not a bit tamed, I too am untranslatable, / I sound my barbaric yawp over the roofs of the world." Or again as Whitman has it in one of the reviews of himself: "Self-reliant, with haughty eyes, assuming to himself all the attributes of his country, steps Walt Whitman into literature, talking like a man unaware that there was ever hitherto such a production as a book, or such a being as a writer. Every move of him has the free play of the muscle of one who never knew what it was to feel that he stood in the presence of a superior" (*In Re Walt Whitman*, p. 14)—and, we might add, one who never knew what it was to feel the constraints, however slight, of any traditional metrical form. But what he did feel, and what we must feel in reading him, was the line, the shape of the line, cast out in an arc to the precise right length as an expert fly-fisherman might cast out a line. When Henry James says of the poems in *Drum Taps* that "[e]ach line starts off by itself, in resolute independence of its companions, without a visible goal," he is about one-quarter right, for Whitman's lines do have a wonderful integrity about them— that is the one-quarter—but the Whitmanian line is not resolutely independent of its companions, quite the contrary (which is why, once started, one can hardly stop reading Whitman), nor is it without visible goal, which is often enough virtual repetition of itself.

Only by reading Whitman at considerable length, as in "Song of Myself" or "Crossing Brooklyn Ferry" or "Out of the Cradle Endlessly Rocking" or "As I Ebb'd with the Ocean of Life" or "When Lilacs Last in the Dooryard Bloom'd," can one gain a sense of his mastery of the line and of lines themselves rhythmically ordered into a whole poem, but I will try to demonstrate as briefly as I can from a couple of these poems what I understand to be the principles that determine Whitman's rhythms. Here are the first lines of "Out of the Cradle Endlessly Rocking" and "As I Ebb'd with the Ocean of Life," two poems in which the rhythms are clearly Whitman's own while at the same time being intended to suggest the movement of the sea rocking, ebbing, and flowing.

> Out of the cradle endlessly rocking,
> Out of the mocking-bird's throat, the musical shuttle,
> Out of the ninth-month midnight,
> Over the sterile sands and the fields beyond, where the child
>   leaving his bed wander'd alone, bareheaded, barefoot,
> Down from the shower'd halo,
> Up from the mystic play of shadows twining and twisting as if
>   they were alive,
> Out from the patches of briers and blackberries. . . .

And the second poem from "Sea-Drift":

> As I ebb'd with the ocean of life,
> As I wended the shores I know,
> As I walk'd where the ripples continually wash you Paumanok,
> Where they rustle up hoarse and sibilant,
> Where the fierce old mother endlessly cries for her
>   castaways. . . .

There are three preliminary observations that I would make about these lines: first, that I have arbitrarily cut the passages off, for the first seven lines of "Out of the Cradle Endlessly Rocking" are only the beginning of a verse paragraph of twenty-two lines that constitute a single sentence, and the first five lines of "As I Ebb'd with the Ocean of Life" are the beginning of a similar sentence-paragraph of nine lines; second, that none of the lines are run-on in either passage, indeed that there are no run-on lines in either of the poems; and third, that the lines in question establish, right from the beginning, a rhythm proper to this particular poem that will be repeated and endlessly varied throughout the remainder of the poem.

As to the last of these preliminary observations: If we were to scan the first two lines in each of the poems we would get something like this —

> Out of the cradle endlessly rocking,
> Out of the mocking-bird's throat, the musical shuttle. . . .
>
> As I ebb'd with the ocean of life,
> As I wended the shores I know. . . . —

which, employing the terms of traditional prosody, would translate as

> dactyl-trochee, dactyl-trochee,
> dactyl-dactyl-trochee, dactyl-trochee

and

> anapest-anapest-anapest,
> anapest-anapest-iamb.

I do not claim that these prosodic terms do anything like justice to the compelling power of Whitman's rhythms, but they may suggest at any rate how Whitman establishes a rhythmic pattern at the beginning of a poem that is there as an echo in all the variations that follow. Each of the lines in these typical passages is a unit complete in itself but in sense as in rhythmic flow it repeats and completes the lines preceding and following it. How much the lines are complete rhythmic units in themselves is reflected in Whitman's almost total avoidance of enjambment here and everywhere; according to one commentator, only twenty out of more than 10,500 lines in *Leaves of Grass* are run-on.[13] But the rhythmic, syntactic, and sense connections binding any given line to its fellows preceding and following it are as strong as the internal coherence that makes every line a complete unit. Thus the lines, each rhythmically complete in itself, are bound one to another by rhythmic repetition and by syntax and sense into the larger units of verse paragraphs and entire poems. The principle of linear organization in these two poems might be termed "parataxis" — that is, the placing of parallel phrases and clauses one after the other without subordinating or coordinating conjunctions. In the case of "Out of the Cradle Endlessly Rocking" we have twenty-one lines of parallel phrases and clauses before the sentence is finally completed with the verb that is the last word in line twenty-two and the final word of the long, long paratactically organized sentence:

Throwing myself on the sand, confronting the waves,
I, changer of pains and joys, uniter of here and hereafter,
Taking all hints to use them, but swiftly leaping beyond them,
A reminiscence sing.

There are many other things one might say about the rhythms of "Out of the Cradle," but I will content myself with only one, which has to do with the fourteen-line sentence and verse paragraph that follows upon the bird's song. Picking up on the first line of the poem ("Out of the cradle endlessly rocking") and organizing his parataxes as it were from the end of the line rather than the beginning, Whitman concludes every line before the last one with a present participle:

The aria sinking,
All else continuing, the stars shining,

The winds blowing, the notes of the bird continuous echoing,
With angry moans the fierce old mother incessantly moaning,
On the sands of Paumanok's shore gray and rustling,
The yellow half-moon enlarged, sagging down, drooping, the
    face of the sea almost touching,
The boy ecstatic, with his bare feet the waves, with his hair the
    atmosphere dallying,
The love in the heart long pent, now loose, now at last
    tumultuously bursting,
The aria's meaning, the ears, the soul, swiftly depositing,
The strange tears down the cheeks coursing,
The colloquy there, the trio, each uttering,
The undertone, the savage old mother incessantly crying,
To the boy's soul's questions sullenly timing, some drown'd
    secret hissing,
To the outsetting bard.

Whereas the opening lines of the poem display paratactic order
in initial prepositions ("Out of . . . Out of . . . Out of . . . Over . . .
Down from . . . Up from . . . Out from . . ." etc.), the lines in
the post-birdsong passage display a similar parataxis in their final
participles, echoing the "rocking" of line one and creating a kind
of ghostly rhyming effect: "sinking . . . shining . . . echoing . . .
moaning . . . rustling . . . touching . . . dallying . . . bursting . . .
depositing . . . coursing . . . uttering . . . crying . . . hissing," which
brings us to the final short line of the passage: "To the outsetting
bard." I have called this passage a sentence but, as there is no finite
verb in it, it is a sentence only because of the period that closes
it out. Otherwise it has no end but instead has "the fierce old
mother *incessantly* moaning, / . . . the savage old mother *incessantly*
crying," quite like the "cradle *endlessly* rocking." What Whitman
does in these "Sea-Drift" poems by way of wedding his own internal rhythm to the rhythms of the old mother, the rhythms of
the sea, and the rhythms of all of nature is altogether remarkable
and as characteristic as it is remarkable.

For the rhythmic body of Walt Whitman as described in the self-advertising reviews ("One of the roughs" etc.) we could scarcely do better than to glance at his well-known Louisiana poem—a single sentence (at least as Whitman punctuates it) in thirteen lines:

I saw in Louisiana a live-oak growing,
All alone stood it and the moss hung down from the branches,
Without any companion it grew there uttering joyous leaves of
    dark green,
And its look, rude, unbending, lusty, made me think of myself,
But I wonder'd how it could utter joyous leaves standing alone
    there without its friend near, for I knew I could not,
And I broke off a twig with a certain number of leaves upon it,
    and twined around it a little moss,
And brought it away, and I have placed it in sight in my room,
It is not needed to remind me as of my own dear friends,
(For I believe lately I think of little else than of them,)
Yet it remains to me a curious token, it makes me think of
    manly love;
For all that, and though the live-oak glistens there in Louisiana
    solitary in a wide flat space,
Uttering joyous leaves all its life without a friend a lover near,
I know very well I could not.

The question of how a Whitmanian live-oak tree, "rude, unbending, lusty," but "solitary in a wide flat space" in Louisiana, could utter "joyous leaves all its life without a friend a lover near" is one that we might imagine would have been of considerable interest to Emily Dickinson or Gerard Manley Hopkins, both of whom were isolated and "all alone" in ways that Whitman never experienced and would have found intolerable. It is true that the leaves uttered by Dickinson and Hopkins are not always to be described as "joyous," but even with that granted, I wonder if one might not speculate that *pace* Whitman it was precisely their isolation that caused Dickinson and Hopkins to utter leaves at all — or at least that it was their isolation that caused them to utter the particular leaves that they did utter. That question, however, I want to defer until later; here I am concerned with the rhythmic properties that make what Dickinson and Hopkins wrote poetry, if not in the same way nevertheless to the same degree as what Whitman wrote.

Any responsive reader of Emily Dickinson will feel in her poetry a personal rhythm as pronounced as that of Whitman in his poetry. There is, however, this essential difference between them that while Whitman typically displays *only* a personal-natural rhythm without a hint of received meter, Dickinson plays her rhythm off against, and filters it through, certain highly traditional metrical forms, thereby radically reconstituting those traditional meters and, as it were, commenting on them. When I use the phrase "plays her rhythm off against" I do so advisedly, for there is a very large element of play, frequently of an ironic sort, in the rhythmic expression of Dickinson's personality and her poetry. As a number of scholars have pointed out, most of her poems adopt meters from English hymnology; in particular, as Thomas H. Johnson and Martha Winburn England among others have shown, she was from early childhood on thoroughly imbued with, though not at all enamored of, the hymns of Isaac Watts. Those hymns imposed themselves on — and as — Dickinson's metrical consciousness, in such a way that she could hardly escape them when she would herself write poetry. The only escape came in playing off against the received hymn meters and in writing verse that imitated Watts, but imitated him parodically, for if her form was often similar to his, Dickinson's message was very different indeed; and that different message was in part — not entirely, but in very considerable part — conveyed by twisting and turning and torturing the hymnist's meter to suit her own rhythm and her own purposes. Here is a fairly typical Watts hymn against which we might place any number of Dickinson poems:

When I can read my title clear
  To mansions in the skies,
I bid farewell to ev'ry fear,
  And wipe my weeping eyes.

Should earth against my soul engage,
  And hellish darts be hurl'd,
Then I can smile at Satan's rage,
  And face a frowning world.

Let cares, like a wild deluge come,
  And storms of sorrow fall;
May I but safely reach my home,
  My God, my heav'n, my all.

There shall I bathe my weary soul
  In seas of heav'nly rest,
And not a wave of trouble roll
  Across my peaceful breast.[14]

There is little enough to say about this hymn except that it is strikingly like countless other hymns by Watts and by other hymnists
who followed in his line. Reading through a protestant hymnal
one is rather overwhelmed by a stultifying sameness, as if the
hymns were composed of movable, replaceable, reusable parts,
phrases, lines, and half-lines that can be transported from hymn
to hymn without loss of effect. This is especially true of hymns
like "When I Can Read My Title Clear" that are in Common
Meter—that is, quatrain stanzas composed of lines alternately of
eight and six syllables, rhymed abab (though Dickinson, when she
adopts Common Meter, normally rhymes only the second and
fourth lines thus: abcb). Everything about "When I Can Read
My Title Clear" is regular, the rhythm entirely without variation
or variety: te-dum, te-dum, te-dum, te-dum; te-dum, te-dum, te-
dum; etc. Rhymes are exact except for the allowable half-rhyme
of "come" with "home." (Were Watts denied this particular half-

rhyme a number of his hymns would suffer—e.g. "Our God, our help in ages past, / Our hope for years to come, / Our shelter from the stormy blast, / And our eternal home!" But this recurrent rhyme merely emphasizes the reusable aspect of the various elements in his hymns.) Nothing in the hymn provides any resistance or friction that would cause a reader-singer to halt or come up short in reading-singing. Consider, by way of contrast, Dickinson's #744, which, though in the same Common Meter as the Watts hymn, is all friction and resistance, startling in all its parts and impossible to read in the mindless te-dum, te-dum, te-dum, te-dum; te-dum, te-dum, te-dum manner so natural to and so authorized by the Watts hymn:

> Remorse—is Memory—awake—
> Her Parties all astir—
> A Presence of Departed Acts—
> At window—and at Door—
>
> Its Past—set down before the Soul
> And lighted with a Match—
> Perusal—to facilitate—
> And help Belief to stretch—
>
> Remorse is cureless—the Disease
> Not even God—can heal—
> For 'tis His institution—and
> The Adequate of Hell—

One device, of course, by which Dickinson stops readers in their tracks is her signature use of dashes. It would be a hopelessly insensitive reader who could override the dashes to read this as one can perfectly well read a Watts hymn with plenty of religious fervor but little or no trouble to the mind. Leaving aside such other elements as the off-rhymes ("heal" and "Hell" is particularly fine), the special Dickinsonian diction that puts one part of speech for another (e.g., "The Adequate of Hell"), and the stunning thematic beginning ("Remorse—is Memory—awake—")—even without these other stop-you-dead-in-your-tracks elements the dashes by themselves alone serve to establish a nervous, jerky, startled-creature rhythm, specific to Dickinson, that works against, all the while working within, the received Common Meter. The point can be best made perhaps by contrasting the version of this poem as I have given it with the version printed in *The Poems of Emily Dickinson*, edited by Martha Dickinson Bianchi and Alfred Leete Hampson in 1930:

> Remorse is memory awake,
> Her companions astir,—
> A presence of departed acts
> At window and at door.
>
> Its past set down before the soul,
> And lighted with a match,
> Perusal to facilitate
> Of its condensed despatch.
>
> Remorse is cureless,—the disease
> Not even God can heal;
> For 'tis His institution,—
> The complement of hell.

Not only have the editors removed most of the dashes, so that the poem flows much more smoothly and blandly in a Wattslike manner, but they have shown a sure sense of wrong editorial choices when faced with optional readings in lines 2, 8, and 12 (especially deplorable is the choice of "complement" rather than "Adequate") and when they decided to drop the very effective "and" in line 11.

We can find a similar playing-off-against principle at work in the relatively early poem #193 where Dickinson appears to waver between loyalty to traditional hymnic meter[15] and her own experiential rhythm, but what she really does, I believe, is to set the hymn up in perfect order in the first stanza only to undercut it entirely and show that it has nothing of use to offer us in the second stanza.

> I shall know why—when Time is over—
> And I have ceased to wonder why—
> Christ will explain each separate anguish
> In the fair schoolroom of the sky—
>
> He will tell me what "Peter" promised—
> And I—for wonder at his woe—
> I shall forget the drop of Anguish
> That scalds me now—that scalds me now!

The first stanza, with its "fair schoolroom of the sky" (compare Watts's "When I can read my title clear / To mansions in the skies") would make fine fodder for the poets' corner of the local newspaper or, more to the point, for the church bulletin or hymnbook that would correspond in poetic virtue to the poets' corner; and it is so blandly rendered that we do not pause over the second line—"And I have ceased to wonder why"—which, were it not all so regular, might catch at our attention and cause us to ask questions: Why should Christ undertake to explain, when the sufferer no longer wonders why? Is this insistence on explaining just another instance of his wanting to tell about his woes in a self-aggrandizing way and at the same time heap more coals on the speaker's head? If the first stanza does not encourage this sort of questioning, however, the second stanza demands it. The peculiar Dickinsonian trick of inverted commas around Peter stops the easy flow of the verse, as does the off-rhyme of "woe" and "now" and, especially, the searing repetition in the last line. In the second stanza there is no "fair schoolroom of the sky" existing in the sweet by-and-by of the hereafter. Rather, there is the seemingly fictitious "Peter," offering promises that may be false; there is the "woe" that, by the rhyme, is "now" and not something to be explained when "I have ceased to wonder why"; and there is the entirely present-tense "Anguish" whose reality and intensity, as against the comforting myth of the hereafter in the first stanza, is emphasized by the repetition and the exclamation point that burns it in: "That scalds me now — that scalds me now!" The poem cited earlier to give some sense of Dickinson's special blend of a personal rhythm and hymnic meter — "I died for Beauty" — is not only in the Common Meter of so many hymns but also, like "I shall know why, when time is over," treats of a subject frequently encountered in the hymn tradition: the fate of the individual soul after death. But how very different it is from the "mansions in the skies" and the Promised Land of the hymns; and how different from Watts's "There shall I bathe my weary soul / In seas of heav'nly rest, / And not a wave of trouble roll / Across my peaceful breast" is the utter annihilation of the individual at the end of Dickinson's poem:

> And so as Kinsmen, met a Night —
> We talked between the Rooms —
> Until the Moss had reached our lips —
> And covered up — our names —

The jarring falling-away from the expected rhyme at the end creates a bathetic effect, an anticlimax where one anticipates, from the traditional form, an exact rhyme and a triumphant climax and closure, a closure denied by the final dash. Dickinson's slant rhyme reflects her slant relationship to both the form and the content of the Watts tradition, and the entire poem constitutes an ironic commentary on the world of the hymns, a commentary that is at once formal and thematic.

Much the same could be said of the use of Common Meter, but in a halting, dash-ridden way and with slant rhymes, in #465:

> I heard a Fly buzz — when I died —
> The Stillness in the Room
> Was like the Stillness in the Air —
> Between the Heaves of Storm —

The Eyes around—had wrung them dry—
And Breaths were gathering firm
For that last Onset—when the King
Be witnessed—in the Room—

I willed my Keepsakes—Signed away
What portion of me be
Assignable—and then it was
There interposed a Fly—

With Blue—uncertain stumbling Buzz—
Between the light—and me—
And then the Windows failed—and then
I could not see to see—

The King expected in the hymns, the King in his Glory, Jesus enthroned in Paradise, is here displaced by the Fly (which rhymes only very dimly with "be"), a fly with "uncertain stumbling Buzz," not unlike the deliberately uncertain, stumbling gait of the poem. One of Isaac Watts's hymns on this same ultimate subject bears a prefatory note that cites the scriptural text and adds an interpretation: "The Song of Simeon: Luke ii.28. Or, a sight of Christ makes death easy." In the hymn itself ("Now have our hearts embrac'd our God")[16] we hear Simeon singing of that which makes death easy for him:

Here we have seen thy face, O Lord,
And view'd salvation with our eyes,
Tasted and felt the living word,
The bread descending from the skies.

In yet another hymn the sight of Christ's face makes death both delightful and desirable:

Jesus! the vision of thy face
    Hath overpow'ring charms!
Scarce shall I feel death's cold embrace,
    If Christ be in my arms.[17]

In Dickinson's poem, however, the dying person is not rewarded with a vision of the King's blessed face, nor is she received into a place of bright light and joyous song with the saints all gathered around the throne. Instead she suffers blindness squared and intensified: not only is she deprived of her vision, not only can she not see, she cannot even "see to see." And yet this state of blind unknowingness, this profound vision of nonvision that spells out a most radical skepticism, is offered to us in the Common Meter of a good little child singing in Sunday school.

One suffers from an embarrassment of riches in any attempt to demonstrate the uses to which Emily Dickinson put the hymn meters of Isaac Watts and his fellow hymnists—uses quite unknown to those more stalwart Christians who often provided Dickinson with her form but seldom her content and almost never her tone. In poem #280 ("I felt a Funeral, in my Brain") she employs once again the good old Common Meter not for one of those subjects that might be found listed in a hymnal—"Comfort," "Eternal Life," "Faith," "God—Majesty and Power of," "Heaven," "Repentance," "Thankfulness," and so on—but as a meter ironically appropriate for rendering the interior drama of incipient madness.

> I felt a Funeral, in my Brain,
> And Mourners to and fro
> Kept treading—treading—till it seemed
> That Sense was breaking through—
>
> And when they all were seated,
> A Service, like a Drum—
> Kept beating—beating—till I thought
> My Mind was going numb—
>
> And then I heard them lift a Box
> And creak across my Soul

> With those same Boots of Lead, again,
> Then Space—began to toll,
>
> As all the Heavens were a Bell,
> And Being, but an Ear,
> And I, and Silence, some strange Race
> Wrecked, solitary, here—
>
> And then a Plank in Reason, broke,
> And I dropped down, and down—
> And hit a World, at every plunge,
> And Finished knowing—then—

It is necessary to read the sense against the meter in #280, refusing to yield to the possibility of singsong that Common Meter always holds; yet, at the same time, the sense is, to an extraordinary degree, *carried* by the rhythm—"A Service, like a Drum— / Kept beating—beating—till I thought / My Mind was going numb—". There is a specific meter but also a more general rhythm at work here, the two crossing and at odds with one another. The heavy beats of "beating—beating" (and in the previous stanza of "treading—treading") are like numbness itself. The poem is more than usually dependent on sounds that, as it were, imitate their meaning. The *t*'s, the *k*'s, the *d*'s, the *p*'s, and especially the *b*'s of the poem ("Brain," "beating—beating," "Box," "Boots," "Bell") are like so many little explosions that, joined to the hallucinatory, auditory images of "creak across my Soul" and "Then Space— began to toll, / As all the Heavens were a Bell, / And Being, but an Ear," render a sense of psychological suffocation and violence, concluding in the psychic implosion of the last stanza. Here, as in half a hundred other poems, Dickinson is almost endlessly resourceful in finding ways to jar and wrench and skewer and stretch the hymn meters that were so natural to her for poetic expression but that would have been of virtually no value to her at all without the treatment to which she subjected them.

Although they were both originals and innovators in their widely different rhythmic practices, neither Dickinson nor Whitman ever had much to say about prosody; neither of them, that is, gave a reasoned account of the principles or the theory of their versification. Dickinson might be said to do so elliptically by her practice as she compels the reader to break up the regularity of Common Meter with her dashes, slant rhymes, enjambed lines, and so on, but she never elaborates her prosodic principles in the form of an explainable, explained system. She just does it. Likewise with Whitman—he never apologizes, never explains. Instead he says, in effect, look at me—"there is that lot of me and all so luscious"—look at me and read me and you will know all you need to know about my rhythmical theories, about my prosody, and about my artless art. Not so Hopkins, who once remarked that he had a passion for explanation. Whether in undergraduate essays, or in notes for lectures on "Rhythm and the other structural parts of Rhetoric" and on "Poetry and verse," or in letters to Robert Bridges and Richard Watson Dixon, or in the preface that he wrote to accompany the manuscript poems he sent to Bridges, Hopkins is forever explaining his ideas on prosody. He planned a book on Greek meters (which, like so many of his projects, came to nothing); and he demonstrated his knowledge of the principles of versification in various traditions by writing prosodically correct poetry (at least what he took to be such) in Greek, Latin, and Welsh. And of course he elaborated a new prosodic principle, which he called "sprung rhythm," and wrote a sizable body of poetry according to that new prosody.

"To speak shortly," Hopkins wrote to Richard Watson Dixon of sprung rhythm—and this is what I would like to do also, to speak shortly—"it consists in scanning by accents or stresses alone, without any account of the number of syllables, so that a foot may be one strong syllable or it may be many light and one strong." [18] In both classical prosody and English prosody, Hopkins writes in his lecture notes on rhythm, "A *foot* is two or more syllables, running to as many as four or five, grouped about one strong beat"[19] and in what he terms "running rhythm" or "standard rhythm," as distinguished from his own sprung rhythm, the same foot, whether of two, three, or four syllables, is repeated throughout the line and from line to line (with allowable variations in the form of reversed feet or what Hopkins calls "counterpoint"). In "standard rhythm," then, you can have feet of two syllables or three syllables or even four or five syllables, but you could not have a foot of only one syllable nor would you mix these different feet within the line or from line to line. Here is where sprung rhythm differs. Sprung rhythm can have feet of one syllable only, and it can freely mix one-syllable, two-syllable, three-syllable feet—up to seven-syllable feet, he says at one point—within the line and from line to line. And because the scansion of sprung rhythm "runs on without break from the beginning . . . of a stanza to the end and all the stanza is one long strain, though written in lines asunder,"[20] the rhythmical unit of sprung rhythm is not the foot so much as it is the line and not the line any more than it is the stanza or the whole poem. Although he claimed originality for his sprung rhythm, Hopkins acknowledged that other poets had employed it, but, as it were, accidentally, not "as the governing principle of the scansion." On the other hand, according to his claim, "Sprung Rhythm is the most natural of things," since "it is the rhythm of common speech and of written prose, when rhythm is perceived in them" ("Author's Preface," p. 117), and "there are hints of it in music, in nursery rhymes and popular jingles" (*The Correspondence of Gerard Manley Hopkins and Richard Watson Dixon*, p. 14). "But no one," he writes in his explanation to Canon Dixon, "has professedly used it and made it the principle throughout, that I know of. Nevertheless to me it appears, I own, to be a better and more natural principle than the ordinary system, much more flexible, and capable of much greater effects" (*Correspondence of GMH and RWD*, pp. 14–15).

The first poem Hopkins attempted in his new rhythm, which

was his first real poem after seven years of self-imposed silence and also a stunning breakthrough in his creativity, was "The Wreck of the Deutschland," begun in December 1875. "You ask, do I write verse myself," Hopkins wrote to Dixon in 1878, and went on to describe the circumstances of his return to poetry:

> What I had written I burnt before I became a Jesuit and re-solved to write no more, as not belonging to my profession, unless it were by the wish of my superiors; so for seven years I wrote nothing but two or three little presentation pieces which occasion called for. But when in the winter of '75 the Deutschland was wrecked in the mouth of the Thames and five Franciscan nuns, exiles from Germany by the Falck Laws, aboard of her were drowned I was affected by the account and happening to say so to my rector he said that he wished some-one would write a poem on the subject. On this hint I set to work and, though my hand was out at first, produced one. I had long had haunting my ear the echo of a new rhythm which now I realised on paper. (p. 14)

Shades of T. S. Eliot and Paul Valéry, of Heaney and Hazlitt, of Wordsworth and Coleridge: "I had long had haunting my ear the echo of a new rhythm" — themeless, and substanceless, pure rhyth-mic form, awaiting its occasion and the experience it might fit — "a new rhythm which now I realised on paper." I hesitate to say that the wreck of the Deutschland — I mean the historic event not the poem — was a godsend for Hopkins, for that would seem a little too close to blasphemy; but it unquestionably did allow him to bring into real being this new rhythm that was haunting him, this rhythm that was indeed (to borrow Emily Dickinson's word) the "Adequate" of himself. And once the rhythm was realized, once it was no longer a wordless, themeless echo haunting his ear but had become words, phrases, feet, lines, and stanzas, then something was released in Hopkins and a great burst of creativity ensued with "God's Grandeur," "The Starlight Night," "As kingfishers catch fire," "Spring," "The Sea and the Skylark," "In the Valley of the Elwy," "The Windhover," "Pied Beauty," "The Caged Sky-lark," "Hurrahing in Harvest," and "The Lantern out of Doors" all pouring forth in no more than a few months' time. I do not mean to say that all of these poems are in sprung rhythm, for a good many of them are not but are instead, as Hopkins indicated, in "standard rhythm"; as he also indicated, however, standard rhythm in these poems is almost always "counterpointed," and "standard rhythm, counterpointed" is something like a halfway house between regular iambic pentameter lines and full-blown sprung rhythm. The point is that in all these poems Hopkins was bringing out from within himself a rhythm that was his own, that was specific to him, but that was also tied in all sorts of ways to speech rhythms—heightened and intensified in the poetry but speech rhythms nevertheless—and that could find its sources and analogues as well in the English poetic tradition down to Hopkins.

We might well illustrate the new rhythm with the first two stanzas of "The Wreck of the Deutschland." The "Deutschland" stanza is an eight-line stanza with the first line having two stresses (in the second part of the poem this becomes three stresses), the second line three stresses, the third line four stresses, the fourth line three stresses, the fifth line five stresses, the sixth line again five stresses, the seventh line four stresses, and the eighth line six stresses; and of course there can be any number of unstressed syllables in a line.

> Thou mastering me
> God! giver of breath and bread
> World's strand, sway of the sea;
> Lord of living and dead;
> Thou hast bound bones and veins in me, fastened me flesh,
> And after it almost unmade, what with dread,
> Thy doing: and dost thou touch me afresh?
> Over again I feel thy finger and find thee.

> I did say yes
> O at lightning and lashed rod;
> Thou heardst me truer than tongue confess
> Thy terror, O Christ, O God;
> Thou knowest the walls, altar and hour and night:
> The swoon of a heart that the sweep and the hurl of thee
> trod
> Hard down with a horror of height:
> And the midriff astrain with leaning of, laced with fire of stress.

It will be seen that the Hopkinsian new rhythm—and by "Hopkinsian" I mean that it was *his*, he possessed it but it also possessed him [21]—employs all sorts of other rhythmic devices in addition to the one-stress-per-foot principle, the most notable of them being alliteration, assonance, and the most rigorous rhyme in a scheme of ababcbca (Hopkins was proud of his rhymes: "my rhymes are rigidly good—to the ear—and such rhymes as *love* and *prove* I scout utterly," he wrote to Robert Bridges,[22] who had accused him of excessive license in his rhyming). "Besides the bare principle which I have been explaining [that *one stress makes one foot*]," Hopkins wrote to Dixon, "I employ various artifices which you will see in reading" (*Correspondence of GMH and RWD*, p. 23).

What are the virtues of this new rhythm other than that it is Hopkins's very own? As he is the "onlie begetter" of it, Hopkins is himself the best advocate for sprung rhythm ("sprung," he said, "means something like abrupt"), as in this letter to Bridges (*The Letters of Gerard Manley Hopkins to Robert Bridges*, p. 46):

> Why do I employ sprung rhythm at all? Because it is the nearest to the rhythm of prose, that is the native and natural rhythm of speech, the least forced, the most rhetorical and emphatic of all possible rhythms, combining, as it seems to me, opposite and, one wd. have thought, incompatible excellences, markedness of rhythm—that is rhythm's very self—and naturalness of expression—for why, if it is forcible in

prose to say "lashed:rod," am I obliged to weaken this in verse, which ought to be stronger, not weaker, into "lashed birch-rod" or something?

But having claimed for sprung rhythm that it "is the nearest to the rhythm of prose," Hopkins realized on other occasions that he had left himself open on another flank to the charge that, as far as rhythm goes, he was not writing poetry any more than the young Henry James thought Whitman was. Indeed, the accusation that Hopkins was too like Whitman in his rhythms stung him more than once. When Hopkins wrote to Father Henry Coleridge, editor of the Jesuit periodical the *Month*, describing "The Wreck of the Deutschland" (but without sending him a copy of the poem), Coleridge responded, according to Hopkins's account to his mother in a letter, with the rather prescient remark "that there was in America a new sort of poetry which did not rhyme or scan or construe; if mine rhymed and scanned and construed," Hopkins went on, "and did not make nonsense or bad morality he [Coleridge] did not see why it shd. not do" for the journal.[23] That Coleridge should have alluded so clearly to Whitman with his remark about poetry that "did not rhyme or scan or construe" and that he should have suspected Hopkins of Whitmanizing in "The Wreck of the Deutschland" without having seen the poem is somewhat surprising. In any case, when Coleridge did eventually receive a copy of the poem from Hopkins, while he might not have been able to scan or construe it, the poem certainly rhymed, it certainly followed a deliberate and elaborate stanzaic design, and it certainly showed many other properties of poetry about it. Moreover, Hopkins could argue, and did argue, that according to his prosodic principles the poem scanned and construed very well and that it made neither nonsense nor bad morality. Nevertheless, the *Month* eventually declined to publish the poem.

Robert Bridges never liked "The Wreck of the Deutschland" very much, but it was in connection with another, later poem

("The Leaden Echo and the Golden Echo") that Bridges said that Hopkins showed Whitmanian tendencies in his poetry and even, Bridges suggested, the direct influence of Whitman. Hopkins responded to the charge defensively and at a length (four printed pages) that even he considered excessive. In his response Hopkins acknowledges that "there was to the eye something in my long lines like his, that the one would remind people of the other," and he concedes that "both are in irregular rhythms." But this is as far as he will go: "There the likeness ends," Hopkins says.

> The pieces of his I read were mostly in an irregular rhythmic prose: that is what they are thought to be meant for and what they seemed to me to be. . . . [I]n short what he means to write — and writes — is rhythmic prose and that only. . . . He dreams of no other and he *means* a rugged or, as he calls it, . . . a "savage" art and rhythm.
>
> Extremes meet, and (I must for truth's sake say what sounds pride) this savagery of his art, this rhythm in its last ruggedness and decomposition into common prose, comes near the last elaboration of mine. For that piece of mine is very highly wrought. The long lines are not rhythm run to seed: everything is weighed and timed in them. (*Letters of GMH to RB*, pp. 155–57)

I think no one would deny that Hopkins's poetry is, as he says, "very highly wrought." What he was attempting was like a high-wire act, maintaining his balance on the wire-edge between a language charged with every poetic artifice he could bring to it and a language that had the vigor and the plain virtues of prose.

It was the increased stress and force and vigor that Hopkins felt sprung rhythm was capable of that made it a rhythm much to be sought and one that could discipline and counteract what he perhaps felt was too great a tendency in his verse to a Keatsian or Pre-Raphaelite sensuosity, quaintness, and archaism. "[I]n common rhythm," Hopkins wrote to Dixon, "in which less is made of stress, in which less stress is laid, the slack must be always one or else two syllables, never less than one and never more than two, and in most measures fixedly one or fixedly two, but in sprung rhythm, the stress being more *of* a stress, being more important, allows of greater variation in the slack" (*Correspondence of GMH and RWD*, p. 39). Hopkins believed that sprung rhythm, with its regular irregularity, with its highly elaborated poetic devices that managed to incorporate into themselves the stressed strength of prose, would allow him to avoid the possibility of any singsong regularity (a danger that Dickinson avoids by other, equally effective means); at the same time, taken together with assonance, alliteration, rhyme, and stanzaic design, it would allow him to claim that he was obviously not writing prose in the guise of poetry à la Walt Whitman. The danger of meter is monotony; of free verse it is formlessness. Hopkins attempted to wed the virtues of the one to the virtues of the other while avoiding the vices of either.

If Whitman and Dickinson could never, rhythmically speaking, see eye to eye, nevertheless we might imagine that peace could be made between them, in some kind of ideal world, through Hopkins's rhythmic ideas and practices. In any case, whether they are to be brought to a harmony of understanding that would include any two or all three of them, what Whitman, Dickinson, and Hopkins were about in their very diverse ways was what I have termed a heightened rhythmization of language, a bringing to language of a rhythm specific to the individual, a rhythm from within joined to rhythms of rhetoric, meter, and speech from without, to produce what we think of as the rhythmic poetic voices—the barbaric yawp, the personalized Common Meter, the sprung rhythm—of Walt Whitman, of Emily Dickinson, of Gerard Manley Hopkins. This being the nature of their various achievements, it is not for nothing that we can think of the three of them, equally and together, as precursors of the poetry that was to come in the century after.

CHAPTER TWO

Tropes of Presence,
Tropes of Absence

"Tell all the Truth but tell it slant," Emily Dickinson advises poets — "Success in Circuit Lies." It is one of the special characteristics of the language of poetry that it should always be slant, that it should work by indirection and "in Circuit," and that it should say one thing in order to mean another. Even Walt Whitman, who one might imagine would differ from Dickinson on this matter of the poet's duplicitous use of language, in fact himself raised the idea of indirection to a principle that he insisted should be the way of the New American Poet. Given the great subject of the American nation, Whitman says in the preface to the 1855 edition of *Leaves of Grass*, "[T]he expression of the American poet is to be transcendant and new. It is to be indirect and not direct or descriptive or epic. Its quality goes through these to much more" (*Walt Whitman: Poetry and Prose*, p. 8). Indirection should be the poet's principle, Whitman said at the outset of his career, and thirty-six or thirty-seven years later, taking "A Backward Glance O'er Travel'd Roads," the word he says he would choose to describe the way his "Leaves" work would be "Suggestiveness": "The word I myself put primarily for the description of them as they stand at last, is the word Suggestiveness. I round and finish little, if anything; and could not, consistently with my scheme. The reader will always have his or her part to do, just as much as I have had mine. I seek less to state or display any theme or thought, and more to bring you, reader, into the atmosphere of the theme or thought—there to pursue your own flight" (*Walt Whitman: Poetry and Prose*, pp. 666–67). As Whitman uses the word, "suggestiveness" has two faces to it: one pertains to the poet's indirection, the other to the reader's role in arriving at the truth that the poet tells, but tells only slant. In the end, Dickinson and Whitman, as usual, are about as far apart as they could well be in the way they slant language or pursue indirection—with Hopkins occupying a kind of middle ground between the two American poets—but in all three of them what is at issue is the figural nature, or the metaphorical character, of the language of poetry.

In speaking of the rhythmic properties of poetry I pointed out that prose and ordinary speech, too, have their proper rhythms but that one could say that in various ways the rhythmic propensities inherent in language use are heightened in poetry. Much the same could be said of metaphor. Language itself, as many commentators have pointed out, is metaphoric by nature: it puts one thing for another, it transposes thought into words, it gives names to things of the natural world. Besides this basic metaphoricity of all language, where words are substituted for objects and concepts, there is the common sort of metaphor, a second-level metaphor we might say, that finds resemblance between things and forms words or phrases that enter language on the basis of that resemblance. We find this second-level metaphor in a phrase like "finger of land" or a name like the "Finger Lakes" or an expression such as "to finger someone," in all of which the metaphor remains quite visible: we can "see" (of course I use "see" metaphorically, but this is the point: one is caught in metaphor whenever one uses language) why a "finger of land" or the "Finger Lakes" are called that, and we can easily see or understand the relationship between identifying someone and pointing to them with a finger. A little less obvious, a little more hidden in the language, are such phrases as the "hands of a clock," a horse that stands "eight hands high," or "farmhands"; and less visible still, or less visualizable because it is buried in the language, is a phrase like the "foot of a mountain" or "foothills" (which the dictionary says means "hills at the *foot* of higher hills"). In these expressions we do not "see" a foot in the way we might be said to "see" a finger in the earlier expressions. And buried in double linguistic obscurity is a geographical designation like "Piedmont" (translatable as "foothill" or "mountain-foot"), which for most people, I should think, is simply the name of an area, a name that reveals little or nothing of its metaphoric origins. All of the foregoing are metaphors that one might say are natural to language, as a tendency to rhythm is likewise natural in language use. But just as the language of poetry heightens and intensifies the rhythmic properties inherent in all language, so too does it adopt all the metaphors buried in ordinary language (frequently examining them in such a way as to make them visible again); and at the same time the language of poetry increases the pressure of metaphor, raising it to a third level beyond the two already mentioned. The poet consciously, habitually, and on principle speaks metaphorically, saying one thing to mean another.

Metaphor is always, and in the hands of the poet to an extraordinary degree, a means both of discovery and of creation. It is an act of discovery in that it finds similitudes already existing between words and things and between words and experience; and it is an act of creation in that it projects those similitudes beyond the realm of things and the realm of experience to connect the known with the unknown. Howard Nemerov has written in a splendid essay called "On Metaphor" that the working of metaphor "is like being told: If you really want to see something, look at something else. If you want to say what something is, inspect something that it isn't. It might go further, and worse, than that: if you want to see the invisible world, look at the visible one."[1] Metaphor takes us through, and by means of, the visible world to the invisible, through the known to the unknown, through the physical to the spiritual, and (especially in Emily Dickinson) through the said to the unsayable. When Whitman declares that "the expres-

sion of the American poet is to be transcendant and new," and
yet that it is also "to be indirect and not direct or descriptive or
epic," he means that the expression of the American poet is to
be metaphoric: the subject is to be transcendent but the way to it
is through the immanent world of men and women, nature and
history (hence his lists and catalogues). Likewise when Hopkins
spends page after page in his journal trying to capture the physical appearance of bluebells—"The bluebells in your hand baffle
you with their inscape, made to every sense," he says in one place
(*The Journals and Papers of Gerard Manley Hopkins*, p. 209), and
then proceeds to submit the bluebells to each of his senses, feeling, smelling, tasting them, listening to the sound as he passes his
hand over them and gazing at them long and lovingly as he tries
to draw one—I suppose that we might think that in a Jesuit priest
this apparent nature worship is somewhat misguided; but did not
Hopkins write, some pages earlier in his journal, "I do not think
I have ever seen anything more beautiful than the bluebell I have
been looking at. I know the beauty of our Lord by it" (p. 199)?
As Nemerov says, "If you really want to see something, look at
something else." If you are Hopkins and want to see the beauty
of the Lord, look at a bluebell—touch it also, smell it, taste it,
listen to it—or look at an ashbough, a falcon, or a row of poplars near Binsey. Or again, when Dickinson begins poem #165
with "A *Wounded* Deer—leaps highest—" it is, as so often with her
poems, difficult to say with any certainty what the poem is *about*
(speculatively, I might say that it seems to be about the way sensitive souls hide spiritual wounds with a mirthful exterior, perhaps
also about the effect of painful emotional experience in certain
poets); if one cannot say with assurance what the poem is about,
however, I feel quite confident in saying that it is *not* about a deer,
wounded or otherwise, nor is it about the act of leaping (indeed,
Dickinson is compelled to say in the next line, "I've heard the
Hunter tell—" which suggests, as I imagine is the case, that she
never saw a wounded deer leaping, whether high or not). But here

is the paradox of metaphor: that whatever Dickinson's subject is, it is unsayable for her in any other way than "A *Wounded* Deer— leaps highest—"

I have been speaking more of what metaphor is for the poet than for the reader, but I would recall here what Whitman says about "Suggestiveness" after remarking that he rounds and finishes little, if anything, in *Leaves of Grass*: "The reader will always have his or her part to do, just as much as I have had mine. I seek less to state or display any theme or thought, and more to bring you, reader, into the atmosphere of the theme or thought—there to pursue your own flight." The reader of Dickinson or of Hopkins, like Whitman's reader, always has his or her part to do, and a major part of that part is to make the metaphoric connections that the poet's slant indirections must always leave unstated. The reader is called upon to be imaginative in response to the poet's act of imagination, to see previously hidden similitudes and to sense a network of connections throughout this world and another one not perceived before; and the metaphoric discoveries made in reading—the discovery of what that wounded deer is about—are a good half of the satisfaction, the pleasure, and the illumination to be had from reading poetry.

Having said that poetry by its very nature is metaphoric and that we can see this perhaps especially well in Dickinson, Hopkins, and Whitman, I want to discriminate a little more finely and distinguish between different senses of metaphor because, while we can say that all three employ metaphor in the general sense of putting one thing to stand for another or saying one thing and meaning something else, it is pretty obvious that metaphor as it operates in Whitman is quite different from metaphor in Dickinson, with Hopkins a kind of *tertium quid* between them—while always remaining, nevertheless, neither Whitmanian nor Dickinsonian but very much Hopkinsian and his own kind of metaphorizer. Up to this point I have been using the term "metaphor" as a kind of metaphor for all figures of speech and for all tropes; as someone has said, and as I have been using it, metaphor is the trope of tropes. However, one might usefully turn the categories upside down to observe that there are different kinds of tropes distinguished by literary theorists and rhetoricians and that metaphor, as a specific tropic operation, is one kind—but not the only kind—of trope available to the poet. Thus Kenneth Burke, in his *Grammar of Motives* (pp. 503–17), writes of what he calls "four master tropes"—metaphor, metonymy, synecdoche, and irony; Paul Ricoeur, in *The Rule of Metaphor*, reduces the number and speaks of "three species of tropes—metonymies, synecdoches, and metaphors" (p. 56). In their *Theory of Literature* René Wellek and Austin Warren content themselves with Ricoeur's three species of tropes, and reduce the categories to only two, when they write, "[W]e may divide the tropes of poetry most relevantly into figures of contiguity and figures of similarity. The traditional figures of contiguity are metonymy and synecdoche"; the traditional figure of similarity is metaphor.[2] The figures of contiguity—metonymy and synecdoche—Ricoeur says are based on correlation or correspondence" (metonymy) and on what he calls "connection" (synecdoche), and the figure of similarity, metaphor, he says is based on "resemblance."

Briefly, then, we have three kinds of tropes:[3] metonymy, a figure of contiguity, which works by correlation or correspondence; synecdoche, also a figure of contiguity (and often said to be a special instance of metonymy), which works by connection; and metaphor, a figure of similarity, which works by resemblance. After their discussion of metonymy, Wellek and Warren write, "Recently some bolder conceptions of metonymy as a literary mode have been suggested, even the notion that metonymy and metaphor may be the characterizing structures of two poetic types—poetry of association by contiguity, of movement within a single world of discourse, and poetry of association by comparison, joining a plurality of worlds" (*Theory of Literature*, pp. 184–85). Now with all these ideas of metaphor, metonymy, and synecdoche in mind, I want to suggest that Dickinson's poetry is thoroughly metaphoric, a poetry that works through figures of similarity, resemblance, and "comparison, joining [or failing to join] a plurality of worlds"; that Whitman's poetry is dominated by tropes of metonymy and synecdoche, the two figures of contiguity or of, respectively, correlation and connection; and that Hopkins's poetry is figuratively mixed, sometimes primarily metaphoric, other times metonymic, and at its best a nearly perfect balance of the two. Further, I will argue that because Dickinson's poetry works through figures of similarity and resemblance that are characteristically so deeply hidden and so extreme in their tenuousness as to be indiscernible or unretrievable, it is most often a poetry of loss ruled by tropes of absence; that, on the other hand, because Whitman's poetry works through figures of contiguity and moves within a single world of discourse, it presents us with tropes of presence (but when the synecdochic connection fails then the tropes become tropes of absence and loss); and finally that because Hopkins's poetry works through figures both of contiguity and similarity, of correspondence, connection, and resemblance, it presents us, sometimes in the same poem, sometimes in different poems, with tropes both of presence and of absence, of plenitude and of loss.

I remarked earlier, using the poem that begins with "A *Wounded Deer* — leaps highest — " as an illustration, that it is often difficult to say what Emily Dickinson's poems are "about," and this is especially true of what we might term "poems of definition," i.e., poems in which she attempts to define the nature of certain interior, psychic experiences (and the interior, as she says in one poem [#258], is "Where the Meanings are"). Definition in such poems usually proceeds by way of description, attempting to find likenesses or similitudes for the impalpable and invisible, to discover sensory similarities and resemblances for that which cannot be apprehended through the senses. " 'Twas like a Maelstrom, with a notch," is a typical beginning of one of these poems of definition, and what the reference for "it" might be—what this poem is "about," in other words—sends commentators riding off in all directions at once.

> 'Twas like a Maelstrom, with a notch,
> That nearer, every Day,
> Kept narrowing its boiling Wheel
> Until the Agony
>
> Toyed coolly with the final inch
> Of your delirious Hem—
> And you dropt, lost,
> When something broke—
> And let you from a Dream—
>
> As if a Goblin with a Gauge—
> Kept measuring the Hours—
> Until you felt your Second
> Weigh, helpless, in his Paws—
>
> And not a Sinew—stirred—could help,
> And sense was setting numb—
> When God—remembered—and the Fiend
> Let go, then, Overcome—
>
> As if your Sentence stood—pronounced—
> And you were frozen led
> From Dungeon's luxury of Doubt
> To Gibbets, and the Dead—
>
> And when the Film had stitched your eyes
> A Creature gasped "Reprieve"!
> Which Anguish was the utterest—then—
> To perish, or to live?

"It"—this past experience that leaves the speaker to question whether it were greater anguish to perish in the experience or to survive it—was like a maelstrom with a notch, like seeing your life weighed in a goblin's paws, like being sentenced to death by hanging, like, finally, being reprieved when death might be more of a blessing than the reprieve. So that is what "it" was *like;* what "it" *was* is another matter. Was it agony over a lost love? Was it terror at the prospect of death? Was it incipient madness? All of these have been suggested but they are no more than pale abstractions beside the profoundly metaphoric experience of the poem. But why "maelstrom with a notch"? Outside of Emily Dickinson's poetry, can a maelstrom *have* a notch? In order not to be caught out in this matter and be told that there is a famous notched maelstrom that occurs in the North Sea or somewhere, I consulted the word in the dictionary and found, not indeed what I feared, but something rather interesting. A maelstrom, according to the first dictionary definition, is "a powerful often violent whirlpool sucking in objects within a given radius," which is about what I thought it was; but the second definition, if it can be called a definition, is "something resembling a maelstrom in turbulence." There is something slightly vertiginous in taking this second definition to Dickinson's poem. If you would know what Emily Dickinson's experience was, her poem says, think of a maelstrom with a notch (never mind that you cannot quite visualize it: imagine it); if you would know what a maelstrom is, the dictionary says, think of something like Dickinson's turbulent experience.

The poems that begin " 'Tis so appalling—it exhilirates," "It was not Death, for I stood up," "I felt a Funeral in my Brain," "The First Day's Night had come" (which concludes, "Could it be Madness—this?"), "I felt a Cleaving in my Mind," "After great pain, a formal feeling comes," "He fumbles at your Soul," "There's a certain Slant of light," and many more are structured alike as attempts at describing, defining, realizing psychic experience—which for Dickinson is loss—by way of similes and metaphors. I have termed these "poems of definition," but they might more exactly be called "poems-of-the-impossibility-of-definition," for nearly always there is the sense that they are trying to get at the unsayable. I do not mean, of course, that the poems are failures; on the contrary, the poems mentioned are among Dickinson's assured successes, but they succeed not by saying something but, as it were, by pointing to something else, the metaphors through which the poems' subjects are realized. "The Martyr Poets—did not tell— / But wrought their Pang in syllable—," as Dickinson has it in poem #544. "The Martyr Painters—never spoke— / Bequeathing—rather—to their Work—" There is a certain irony in the fact that in this poem Dickinson states that Martyr Poets do not state; nevertheless, the point remains a valid one that in her best poems statement is replaced by a working of her Pang in syllable and metaphor.

If we think of the metaphoric relationship as being between the known on the one side and the unknown on the other, or between the visible and the invisible, with an essential similarity implied in the terms on either side, then we should have to go on to observe that Dickinson's metaphors are frequently free-floating and unattached on the farther side, so that readers must fill in from their own experience the terms for the unknown and invisible—and as individual experiences vary so, of course, will the terms we fill in as readers. Different commentators on poem #520, "I started Early—Took my Dog—," for example, have felt that the sea, because of its actions and the speaker's response, bears some similarity to and hence can be taken as a metaphor for such disparate, farther-side terms as death, experience, a specific lover or love in general, psychosis, or God, and a few more besides. Here is the poem that evokes these many and various interpretive responses:

> I started Early—Took my Dog—
> And visited the Sea—
> The Mermaids in the Basement
> Came out to look at me—

And Frigates—in the Upper Floor
Extended Hempen Hands—
Presuming Me to be a Mouse—
Aground—upon the Sands—

But no Man moved Me—till the Tide
Went past my simple Shoe—
And past my Apron—and my Belt
And past my Bodice—too—

And made as He would eat me up—
As wholly as a Dew
Upon a Dandelion's Sleeve—
And then—I started—too—

And He—He followed—close behind—
I felt His Silver Heel
Upon my Ankle—Then my Shoes
Would overflow with Pearl—

Until We met the Solid Town—
No One He seemed to know—
And bowing—with a Mighty look—
At me—The Sea withdrew—

There is something eerie, something uncanny and baffling about
a poem like this one that is so dense in felt meaning—but what
is that meaning, what is the poem doing? It is as if the signifier—
in this case the sea—can never meet its signified. Which is not
to say that there *is* no signified, but that whatever it may be it is
prelinguistic, extra-linguistic, nonlinguistic—a terror, a void, a je
ne sais quoi. Metaphor stretches out and fails to find the term on
the other side, yet it does its work of suggestiveness. The reader
knows that what language and metaphor strain toward, yet fail to
reach, is a reality—and knows it, paradoxically, by the poem. This
same eerie bafflement, which starts as the technique of the poem

and becomes its subject, we find again and again in Dickinson, for example in poem #510:

> It was not Death, for I stood up,
> And all the Dead, lie down—
> It was not Night, for all the Bells
> Put out their Tongues, for Noon.
>
> It was not Frost, for on my Flesh
> I felt Siroccos—crawl—
> Nor Fire—for just my Marble feet
> Could keep a Chancel, cool—
>
> And yet, it tasted, like them all,
> The Figures I have seen
> Set orderly, for Burial,
> Reminded me, of mine—
>
> As if my life were shaven,
> And fitted to a frame,
> And could not breathe without a key,
> And 'twas like Midnight, some—
>
> When everything that ticked—has stopped—
> And Space stares all around—
> Or Grisly frosts—first Autumn morns,
> Repeal the Beating Ground—
>
> But, most, like Chaos—Stopless—cool—
> Without a Chance, or Spar—
> Or even a Report of Land—
> To justify—Despair.

"It"—how much Dickinson makes of the simple, two-letter word. The overwhelming negativity of this poem, saying what "it" is by saying what it is not and yet is "like"—it is not death, it is not night, it is not frost, it is not fire, yet is "like them all"—is aston-

ishing, and astonishingly effective. The subject itself is a state of
negativity that Dickinson characterizes by a series of negatives,
which, however, she turns at the same time to positive, similitudi-
nous effect. It is a psychic state of "notness," of void, of emptiness
and absence that the poem would describe. "When everything
that ticked—has stopped— / And Space stares all around—": The
poem evokes a terrifying nothingness, and if the stopping here
can be taken as a negative—the negative of continuation—then
the "Stopless" of the final stanza is a kind of double negative, a
way of saying "non-non-continuation." It is negatives heaped on
negatives adding up to nothing—and to a poem capable of making
the reader's flesh, like Siroccos, "crawl." All this "notness" is but
a metaphor for a state of the soul. We look without for a reflection of what is within and see nothing: "'tis as if our Souls /
Absconded—suddenly—" (#645).

Dickinson's is overwhelmingly a poetry of loss, of absence,
of spiritual and psychological void. The important point beyond
this, however, and one to be insisted upon, is that in embracing loss, often embracing it ecstatically, Dickinson transforms the
traumas of emotional experience into the triumph of her poetry.
The vision, however, is one of extremity, nor will Dickinson stop
halfway or offer any comfortable nostrums to readers who might
prefer to have it otherwise. The poem that begins "That after
Horror—that 'twas *us*—" (#286) concludes with these lines about
a sudden near encounter with death and beyond:

> The possibility—to pass
> Without a Moment's Bell—
> Into Conjecture's presence—
> Is like a Face of Steel—
> That suddenly looks into ours
> With a metallic grin—
> The Cordiality of Death—
> Who drills his Welcome in—

The lines suggest that when we come suddenly or at last into the ultimate presence, the presence of that which we conjecture to be, it will turn out to be sheer absence, the absence of death, of annihilation, and no more. When we come at last into God's presence, when we see face to face even as also we are seen, we will be looking upon the blank face of absence.[4] As Dickinson puts it in a letter to T. W. Higginson describing her family, "They are religious—except me—and address an Eclipse, every morning—whom they call their 'Father.'" (*Letters*, #261). The entire question of presence and absence, as played out in Dickinson's poems (and not only there but equally in Whitman and Hopkins) is a fascinating one, nor should this be unexpected since what is at issue in the use of figurative language, and in metaphor in particular, is the change and interchange of terms of presence and absence.

Here we should distinguish again the operation of different kinds of tropes. Metonymy and synecdoche are tropes of contiguity and of proximity; metaphor, by contrast, is a trope of distance. Metaphor asserts a hidden, or heretofore unperceived, similarity between two terms normally taken to be at a distant remove from one another. "I felt a Funeral, in my Brain": All of us have experienced funerals, of course, and I suppose that after reading poem #280 we are ready enough to see how incipient madness, which most of us have not experienced, might be imagined as being like a funeral in the brain, a bizarre funeral, let it be said, in which mourners keep treading, treading, a service like a drum keeps beating, beating, and the coffin is borne by pallbearers shod in boots of lead; at which point in the poem the images and metaphors themselves go mad:

> Then Space—began to toll,
>
> As all the Heavens were a Bell,
> And Being, but an Ear,
> And I, and Silence, some strange Race
> Wrecked, solitary, here—

With space and the heavens likened to a bell and being likened to
an ear, with the speaker of the poem become shipwrecked, alone
in a desolate land with only silence and some strange race around
her, it becomes virtually impossible to hold on to the metaphors
and to recover the sense of them. Madness, as the subject of the
poem, has become also its metaphoric technique. The essential
point I would make, however, is that after reading poem #280
we are able to see that a funeral can be an altogether effective
metaphor for going mad—but we would scarcely have seen any
similarity or thought of the likeness *before* reading the poem. What
we have in the poem, then, is a heretofore unperceived likeness
that gives us some sense or knowledge of a heretofore unknown
experience.

The poet employs metaphor to give presence to that which is,
or has been, absent, thus creating in the poem what I will call an
"absent presence."[5] Through metaphor that which is physically
absent is given a spiritual or meaningful presence. To distinguish
again between the effects of different kinds of tropes, I should say
that metaphor, at its most potent and successful, asserts and establishes an absent presence—a presence for things absent; when it
fails, or when the vision drives the poet to this, as I believe her
vision did Dickinson, then the metaphorizer is left simply, starkly
with the void, an absent absence—nothing on the other side of the
metaphors, which are thus metaphors of loss. Metonymy, on the
other hand, at its most potent and successful, asserts and establishes a present presence, a presence in those things close at hand,
as Whitman does with his lists and catalogues; when metonymy
fails, however, or when the vision drives the poet to this, then the
metonymizer is left tragically not with a void but with a meaningless material world, a present absence, an absence in things all too
much present. Curiously, Dickinson describes an instance of this
latter state of present absence (not, however, through metaphors)
in poem #863:

> That Distance was between Us
> That is not of Mile or Main—
> The Will it is that situates—
> Equator—never can—

This is an unusual instance in Dickinson, however, and I cite it mostly for its value as a curiosity. What we find much more characteristically in her metaphors is that, seeking to give presence to that which is absent, Dickinson discovers that that which is absent is sheer absence, loss and the void, so that what her metaphors give presence to, paradoxically, is in fact absence. But they are undoubtedly successful, terrifyingly successful, in doing that— in giving presence to absence. Consider the difference between despair and fear in poem #305:

> The difference between Despair
> And Fear—is like the One
> Between the instant of a Wreck—
> And when the Wreck has been—
>
> The Mind is smooth—no Motion—
> Contented as the Eye
> Upon the Forehead of a Bust—
> That knows—it cannot see—

I take it that reasons of meter (this is our old friend Common Meter) compelled Dickinson to reverse the analogical terms of the first stanza—i.e., I assume that fear corresponds to the instant of a wreck and despair to when the wreck has been and that the second stanza presents a metaphor for the condition of despair. In the state of despair, the mind is numb and motionless, utterly resigned, like the eye on a bust, to being incapable of that which is its very raison d'être—to see for the eye, to be aware, to be alive, to know for the mind. If the eye could see, what it would see is that it does not see; if the mind could know, what it would know is that it does not know. The great expression of presence as absence is poem #341:

> After great pain, a formal feeling comes—
> The Nerves sit ceremonious, like Tombs—
> The stiff Heart questions was it He, that bore,
> And Yesterday, or Centuries before?
>
> The Feet, mechanical, go round—
> Of Ground, or Air, or Ought—
> A Wooden way
> Regardless grown,
> A Quartz contentment, like a stone—
>
> This is the Hour of Lead—
> Remembered, if outlived,
> As Freezing persons, recollect the Snow—
> First—Chill—then Stupor—then the letting go—

The Quartz contentment here, "like a stone," echoes the state of the mind of poem #305—"Contented as the Eye / Upon the Forehead of a Bust— / That knows—it cannot see—,"—pointing in both instances to utter vacancy. The similitude of the last lines, comparing "the Hour of Lead" (already a pretty compacted metaphor) to the experience of people frozen to a state beyond life but just short of death, presents much the same condition of psychic nullity and death-in-life as we have in "It was not Death, for I stood up" (#510) and so many more Dickinson poems.

In poem #744 it is memory that is responsible for giving presence—in this case unwanted presence—to experiences removed in time:

> Remorse—is Memory—awake—
> Her Parties all astir—
> A Presence of Departed Acts—
> At window—and at Door—

One has the eerie feeling that due to the power of memory, which the speaker would be glad to be freed of, the parties are still going on: though the Acts are Departed, their Presence is undiminished. And there is no remedy, for memory and the remorse that implacably accompanies it, are alike a part of God's ordinance:

> Remorse is cureless — the Disease
> Not even God — can heal —
> For 'tis His institution — and
> The Adequate of Hell —

The metaphor of these last lines is astonishing, thoroughly Dickinsonian, and altogether blasphemous. Remorse (which equals "Memory — awake") is a disease, ordained by God to be the very heart of the human condition and therefore incurable by Him or anyone else, and the "Adequate of Hell": We are each of us our own Hell, nor are we out of it, nor can we ever be out of it, and it is all God's doing.

A more cheerful version of the Dickinsonian void can be found in poem #605 where the activity of the spider is offered as a metaphor for the creativity of the poet and artist:

> The Spider holds a Silver Ball
> In unperceived Hands —
> And dancing softly to Himself
> His Yarn of Pearl — unwinds —
>
> He plies from Nought to Nought —
> In unsubstantial Trade —
> Supplants our Tapestries with His —
> In half the period —
>
> An Hour to rear supreme
> His Continents of Light —
> Then dangle from the Housewife's Broom —
> His Boundaries — forgot —

As in poem #512, where "The Soul has Bandaged moments" of sheer horror but also "has moments of Escape— / When bursting all the doors— / She dances like a Bomb, abroad, / And swings upon the Hours," the plight of the human being and especially of the artist is not one of unrelieved misery nor is it "the Adequate of Hell." The spider has his moments, and they are very attractive moments, of holding "a Silver Ball" and "dancing softly to Himself," and the poem conveys a sense of glorying in such creative moments. But we should not fail to see that such moments are transient and ephemeral, and we must note that the spider, together with his creation, ends up dangling "from the Housewife's Broom— / His Boundaries—forgot—" I take "Boundaries" to be a synonym for Dickinson's great word "Circumference," the word in which she figures the outer reaches of human endeavor touched on in her poetry ("My Business is Circumference," she declared in a letter to Higginson [#268]), and if this is correct then by the end of the poem, "Boundaries" and "Circumference" are "forgot"—absent altogether. Moreover, lovely as the phrase "dancing softly to Himself" may be, we are told in the middle stanza that the spider "plies from Nought to Nought"—connecting "Nothing with nothing" like the Thames daughter in *The Waste Land*—"In unsubstantial Trade." What is so glorious in the first stanza is sharply qualified in the second stanza and virtually destroyed in the third. Thus the fate of the spider and his web in Dickinson.

How differently the creative soul and the "noiseless patient spider" fare in Whitman's poem:

A noiseless patient spider,
I mark'd where on a little promontory it stood isolated,
Mark'd how to explore the vacant vast surrounding,
It launch'd forth filament, filament, filament, out of itself,
Ever unreeling them, ever tirelessly speeding them.

And you O my soul where you stand,
Surrounded, detached, in measureless oceans of space,
Ceaselessly musing, venturing, throwing, seeking the spheres to
    connect them,
Till the bridge you will need be form'd, till the ductile anchor
    hold,
Till the gossamer thread you fling catch somewhere, O my soul.

Though the spider explores a "vacant vast surrounding" and the "oceans of space" in which the soul stands are "measureless," nevertheless Whitman is confident in either case that the needed bridge will be formed and that the ductile anchor will catch and hold. There is seldom any comparable confidence in Dickinson who plies from nought to nought with an anchor that cannot hold because there is nothing to hold to. One way of describing their poetic practices is to say that Dickinson is a poet of metaphor, Whitman a poet of metonymy and synecdoche, and this makes all the difference. John Berryman, contrasting Whitman with T. S. Eliot in an essay in *The Freedom of the Poet*, writes, "The poet as creator plays no part in Whitman's scheme at all" (p. 230). This comes at first as something of a shock, but taken in context and especially if one thinks of the relationship between Dickinson and Whitman, it makes very good sense. Whitman's entire project, as he himself says in "A Backward Glance O'er Travel'd Roads," was "an attempt, from first to last, to put *a Person*, a human being (myself, in the latter half of the Nineteenth Century, in America,) freely, fully and truly on record." As Berryman says, Whitman was a recorder not a maker; his effort was not to create where there was nothing, but rather to record and to celebrate what was plainly already there. Dickinson, by contrast, is par excellence a maker, a creator of worlds — linguistic worlds they may be, but in any case they did not come to her, as did the world for Whitman, as something already made and in existence. And Whitman's is a world of plenitude—at least he declares it to be so—while Dickinson's is a world of vacancy and absence. Her metaphors would join, through similarities, worlds that are distant one from another; his metonymies and synecdoches discover correlations and connections in a world that is proximate, contiguous, and of a piece.

I have remarked of a poem like Dickinson's #165 ("A *Wounded Deer*—leaps highest") that it is frequently difficult to say what it is about; the same is seldom true of Whitman's poems, for the subject is there at hand. "Song of Myself," "I Sing the Body Electric," "Spontaneous Me," "So Long!"—one does not have to seek long or far, or exercise great ingenuity, to discover the subjects of these poems. Whitman is forever setting out in *Leaves of Grass* to take in the scene around him. "Taking in the scene around him": I want to look rather closely at this commonplace expression I have just used. The poems present Whitman as doing this in a literal way, taking in, taking into himself, the scene around him—touching, embracing, devouring, absorbing everyone and everything he encounters, gazing voyeuristically and with such intensity that he becomes what he sees. But what Whitman offers to us in literal terms we are to understand, I believe, as a metonym for his relationship to (in D. H. Lawrence's phrase) "the circumambient universe." In "The Sleepers," for example, Whitman declares:

> I wander all night in my vision,
> Stepping with light feet, swiftly and noiselessly stepping and
>   stopping,
> Bending with open eyes over the shut eyes of sleepers. . . ,
> Pausing, gazing, bending, and stopping. . . .
> I stand in the dark with drooping eyes by the worst-suffering
>   and the most restless,
> I pass my hands soothingly to and fro a few inches from them,
> The restless sink in their beds, they fitfully sleep. . . .

I go from bedside to bedside, I sleep close with the other
  sleepers each in turn,
I dream in my dream all the dreams of the other dreamers,
And I become the other dreamers. . . .
I am the actor, the actress, the voter, the politician. . . .

and so on: there follows one of those lists so characteristic of
Whitman, this time a list of all the sleepers he looks on and becomes. What are all those lists but a cataloguing and recording of
the visible universe that lies about him and that Whitman takes
in as he catalogues and records it? "The known universe has one
complete lover and that is the greatest poet," Whitman declared
in the preface to the 1855 *Leaves of Grass*. And further of the great
poet and the great poem:

> The greatest poet does not moralize or make applications of
> morals . . . he knows the soul. . . . The greatest poet has
> less a marked style and is more the channel of thoughts and
> things without increase or diminution, and is the free chan-
> nel of himself. . . . Extreme caution or prudence, the soundest
> organic health, large hope and comparison and fondness for
> women and children, large alimentiveness. . . , with a per-
> fect sense of the oneness of nature and the propriety of the
> same spirit applied to human affairs . . . these are called up of
> the float of the brain of the world to be parts of the greatest
> poet. . . . The proof of a poet is that his country absorbs him
> as affectionately as he has absorbed it.[6]

Absorbing and being absorbed, a large alimentiveness, a healthy
appetite for taking in all things and all people as they are — these
are the trademark characteristics of Whitman's great poet and,
not surprisingly, of the poems in *Leaves of Grass*.

What Whitman intended, of course, in cataloguing America
and Americans and simultaneously putting "*a Person*, a human

The Language(s) of Poetry

being (myself. . .) freely, fully and truly on record," was to line
the two up, Walt Whitman and the American nation, so that they
would be seen to be identical, and identical not just at a moment in
the nineteenth century but on into the future one hundred years
hence as Whitman claims in "Crossing Brooklyn Ferry." "Closer
yet I approach you," Whitman says to the person he imagines
crossing the East River on the Brooklyn Ferry "a hundred years
hence, or ever so many hundred years hence,"

> Closer yet I approach you,
> What thought you have of me now, I had as much of you —
>   I laid in my stores in advance,
> I consider'd long and seriously of you before you were born.
>
> Who was to know what should come home to me?
> Who knows but I am enjoying this?
> Who knows, for all the distance, but I am as good as looking
>   at you now, for all you cannot see me? . . .
>
> What is more subtle than this which ties me to the woman or
>   man that looks in my face?
> Which fuses me into you now, and pours my meaning into you?

This is all present tense as Whitman, through the power of his
imagination, absorbs those who cross by the Brooklyn Ferry in
the future and is himself absorbed by the reader in the act of reading. The scene is present to Whitman as the world was present to
him. And the same mutually absorptive relationship is projected
into the future as well in the address to the reader at the end of
"Song of Myself":

> I bequeath myself to the dirt to grow from the grass I love,
> If you want me again look for me under your boot-soles.
>
> You will hardly know who I am or what I mean,
> But I shall be good health to you nevertheless,
> And filter and fibre your blood.

Failing to fetch me at first keep encouraged,
Missing me one place search another,
I stop somewhere waiting for you.

Whitman's reader is to be as largely alimentive as the poet himself, with the chief nourishment being the poet's body and the
body of his poem. "Song of Myself" begins with "I" ("I celebrate
myself, and sing myself") and it ends with "you" ("I stop somewhere waiting for you"): Whitman's body has been absorbed into
the body of America, into the body of the world, into the body of
his readers.

Whitman had an appetite for things greater even than the
American nation; indeed, his alimentiveness was more than large,
it was insatiable. "I am large, I contain multitudes," as he famously
says in "Song of Myself" (section 51). "I am an acme of things
accomplish'd, and I an encloser of things to be" (section 44). He
was a part of the American nation and of the circumambient universe but he was also, in imaginative projection, their center and
their circumference:

I open my scuttle at night and see the far-sprinkled systems,
And all I see multiplied as high as I can cipher edge but the rim
    of the farther systems.

Wider and wider they spread, expanding, always expanding,
Outward and outward and forever outward.
                                    ("Song of Myself," section 45)

Lying at the center of vast cosmic systems, "the greatest poet," he
of the largest alimentiveness who has shortly before this declared
himself a "kosmos," is able to surround those systems with his
consciousness and so draw them into himself.

Ceaselessly musing, venturing, throwing, seeking the spheres
    to connect them,

Till the bridge you will need be form'd, till the ductile anchor
  hold,
Till the gossamer thread you fling catch somewhere, O my soul.

Identifying himself as poet and part with the wholes of the American nation and the universe, and identifying those wholes with
himself as the supremely conscious central part, is not Whitman
enacting a kind of textbook definition of synecdoche — a figure of
speech that takes the part for the whole or the whole for the part?
"The 'noblest synecdoche,'" Kenneth Burke writes in his "Four
Master Tropes" essay, "the perfect paradigm or prototype for
all lesser usages, is found in metaphysical doctrines proclaiming
the identity of 'microcosm' and 'macrocosm.' In such doctrines,
where the individual is treated as a replica of the universe, and vice
versa, we have the ideal synecdoche, since microcosm is related
to macrocosm as part to whole, and either the whole can represent the part or the part can represent the whole. (For 'represent'
here we could substitute 'be identified with')."[7] When he declared
himself a "kosmos," Whitman didn't specify whether micro- or
macro-, nor did he need to, since, as Burke says, the synecdochic
relationship is perfectly symmetrical and reversible, "either the
whole can represent the part or the part can represent the whole."

I suggested earlier that as poetry that is primarily metaphoric
attempts to give presence to things absent, so poetry that is primarily metonymic attempts to give presence to things present.
Metonymic poetry would spiritualize the material world, whose
reality and presentness it in no way calls into question. This is
undoubtedly what Whitman intended, and believed that he had
accomplished, in *Leaves of Grass*. "The greatest poet," he says in
the 1855 preface,

> hardly knows pettiness or triviality. If he breathes into any
> thing that was before thought small it dilates with the gran-
> deur and life of the universe. He is a seer . . . he is indi-
> vidual . . . he is complete in himself . . . the others are as good

as he, only he sees it and they do not. . . . What the eyesight does to the rest he does to the rest. Who knows the curious mystery of the eyesight? The other senses corroborate themselves, but this is removed from any proof but its own and foreruns the identities of the spiritual world. (*Walt Whitman: Poetry and Prose*, p. 10)

For Whitman the poet is a seer in all senses of the word: he *sees* the physical world in all its presentness, but he also sees—intuits and realizes—its indwelling spiritual essence, and as poet he records both kinds of seeing, thereby spiritualizing and giving presence to the human and physical world. "One main genesis-motive of the 'Leaves,'" Whitman says in his "Backward Glance," "was my conviction (just as strong to-day as ever) that the crowning growth of the United States is to be spiritual and heroic." It was the poet who could see not just the physical grandeur of the United States but its spiritual and heroic character as well.

"O my body!" Whitman exclaims at the beginning of the ninth section of "I Sing the Body Electric," following the exclamation with one of his most detailed catalogues, a catalogue of bodily parts. Except that he starts with the head and works downward rather than from the foot upward, the catalogue is rather like the old song: The toe-bone connected to the foot-bone, the foot-bone connected to the ankle-bone. . . . Now hear the word of the Lord. After listing all his bodily parts, and not scanting even those that others might shy away from ("Ribs, belly, backbone, joints of the backbone, / Hips, hip-sockets, hip-strength, inward and outward round, man-balls, man-root"), Whitman concludes the poem and his celebration of the body and all its parts thus:

> The curious sympathy one feels when feeling with the hand the
>   naked meat of the body,
> The circling rivers the breath, and breathing it in and out,
> The beauty of the waist, and thence of the hips, and thence
>   downward toward the knees,

The thin red jellies within you or within me, the bones and the
   marrow in the bones,
The exquisite realization of health;
O I say these are not the parts and poems of the body only, but
   of the soul,
O I say now these are the soul!

To invest the "parts and poems of the body" with soul, to declare
that the parts and poems of the body *are* the soul—is this not to
confer full presence on that which is fully present? This is what
metonymy is all about and it is what Whitman says very plainly
he intended in *Leaves of Grass*.

But readers have not always understood that Whitman's stock
in trade as a poet was figurative language, in particular metonymy
and synecdoche, instead taking his expressions of "large ama-
tiveness" (as he terms it in the 1855 preface) all too literally as
something like invitations and encouragement to sexual libertin-
ism. At least this is how I read the responses of those like John
Addington Symonds and Anne Gilchrist who seem to have felt
that Whitman was speaking to them not only very personally but
very literally as well about the pleasures of, respectively, homo-
sexual and heterosexual lovemaking. To both of these English
gentlefolk, Whitman wrote in the language that J. Alfred Prufrock imagines the woman using in Eliot's poem: "That is not it
at all, / That is not what I meant, at all." To Anne Gilchrist, who
felt that she could see in Whitman's photograph "the yearning of
thy man-soul toward my woman-soul" (*The Letters of Anne Gilchrist and Walt Whitman*, p. 63), and who herself yearned "with
such passion to soothe and comfort & fill thee with sweet tender
joy" (p. 61), but who made the fatal misstep, as I see it, of writing,
"I am yet young enough to bear thee children, my darling, if God
should so bless me" (p. 66), Whitman finally responded, in fear
that she would turn up on his doorstep (as in fact she eventually
did), "Dear friend, let me warn you somewhat about myself—and

yourself also. You must not construct such an unauthorized and imaginary ideal Figure and call it W. W. and so devotedly invest your loving nature in it. The actual W. W. is a very plain personage and entirely unworthy such devotion" (*The Collected Writings of Walt Whitman: The Correspondence*, II, p. 170). This is backing down very hastily from certain poems that Anne Gilchrist could well be forgiven for having, as Whitman felt, misinterpreted— poems like "A Woman Waits for Me" ("A woman waits for me, she contains all, nothing is lacking, / Yet all were lacking if sex were lacking, or if the moisture of the right man were lacking," etc.[8]) or these lines from "I Sing the Body Electric":

This is the female form,
A divine nimbus exhales from it from head to foot,
It attracts with fierce undeniable attraction,
I am drawn by its breath as if I were no more than a helpless
   vapor, all falls aside but myself and it. . . ,
Mad filaments, ungovernable shoots play out of it, the
   response likewise ungovernable,
Hair, bosom, hips, bend of legs, negligent falling hands all
   diffused, mine too diffused,
Ebb stung by the flow and flow stung by the ebb, love-flesh
   swelling and deliciously aching,
Limitless limpid jets of love hot and enormous, quivering jelly
   of love, white-blow and delirious juice,
Bridegroom night of love working surely and softly into the
   prostrate dawn,
Undulating into the willing and yielding day,
Lost in the cleave of the clasping and sweet-flesh'd day.[9]

Yes, I think Anne Gilchrist might well be forgiven for reading such passages in a literal rather than a metonymic way, and Whitman seems at times to be conscious that he has given her somewhat more than slight encouragement toward such a reading. But he professed not to be able to understand at all how John Addington Symonds could have got it so wrong or why he should have been so confoundedly insistent on getting from Whitman agreement "that, human nature being what it is, and some men having a strong natural bias toward persons of their own sex, the enthusiasm of 'Calamus' is calculated to encourage ardent and *physical* intimacies." After avoiding answering this sort of thing for as long as he could, Whitman finally felt compelled to respond: "Ab't the questions of Calamus pieces &c: they quite daze me . . . that the calamus part [of *Leaves of Grass*] has even allow'd the possibility of such construction as mention'd is terrible — I am fain to hope the pages themselves are not to be even mention'd for such gratuitous and quite at the time entirely undream'd & unreck'd possibility of morbid inferences — wh' are disavow'd by me & seem damnable." After some more comments about *Leaves of Grass* and a description of his present state of health (designed presumably to ward off even the bare possibility of any amative visit from Symonds: "I live here 72 y'rs old & completely paralyzed"), Whitman comes up with one of the great non sequiturs, and probably nontruths, of all time: "Tho' always unmarried I have had six children. . . ." (*Correspondence*, V, pp. 72–73). Further questions about "ardent and *physical* intimacies" between men would be clearly unwelcome and, moreover, Whitman implies, entirely inappropriate. Be that as it may — and I think the rather confused diction and syntax of Whitman's objection to Symonds's reading betray something like a fearful suspicion that Symonds may be coming much too close to the heart of the matter — in their misinterpretations of Whitman, were not Gilchrist and Symonds receiving the full *presentness* of Whitman's subject without a corresponding and sufficient awareness of the *presence* that, by metonymy, Whitman felt he had brought to that presentness?

But Whitman himself at times had doubts, and more than doubts, about whether his synecdoches and metonymies could hold, doubts about whether in fact there was the possibility of any presence about the present at all. In *Democratic Vistas*, after acknowledging the great material prosperity of the United States, Whitman turns to what he sees as a corresponding moral and social poverty in the nation: "[S]ociety, in these States, is canker'd, crude, superstitious, and rotten. . . . Never was there, perhaps, more hollowness at heart than at present, and here in the United States." He follows this with a catalogue, not of the usual celebratory sort, but instead a list of the diseases and corruptions of the American body politic that no muckraker of later years could surpass, and he concludes, "It is as if we were somehow being endow'd with a vast and more and more thoroughly-appointed body, and then left with little or no soul" (*Walt Whitman: Poetry and Prose*, 937–38). True, Whitman speaks hopefully of a future when there will be poet-priests capable of infusing soul into the vast national body, but he did not see the effects of such poet-priests in 1870, and he significantly does not make the claim for himself in *Democratic Vistas*. Within three years of the publication of *Democratic Vistas* Whitman had suffered the paralytic stroke that reduced his own body, heretofore a stout partner in forging his metonymies and synecdoches, to impotence. "A batter'd, wreck'd old man," he says of himself through the persona of Columbus in "Prayer of Columbus,"

> A batter'd, wreck'd old man. . . ,
> Sore, stiff with many toils, sicken'd and nigh to death,
> I take my way along the island's edge,
> Venting a heavy heart. . . .
> My terminus near,
> The clouds already closing in upon me,
> The voyage balk'd, the course disputed, lost,
> I yield my ships to Thee. . . .
> Is it the prophet's thought I speak, or am I raving?
> What do I know of life? what of myself?
> I know not even my own work past or present,
> Dim ever-shifting guesses of it spread before me,

Of new better world, their mighty parturition,
Mocking, perplexing me.

It was not only at the time that his body failed him, however, that Whitman despaired, at least momentarily, of the efficaciousness of the synecdoche that connected his souled body to the souled body of America, not only then that he feared that the one body and the other were hollow and dead. "I too but signify at the utmost a little wash'd updrift," he says in "As I Ebb'd with the Ocean of Life":

> A few sands and dead leaves to gather,
> Gather, and merge myself as part of the sands and drift. . . .
> I too am but a trail of drift and debris,
> I too leave little wrecks upon you, you fish-shaped island. . . .
> Me and mine, loose windrows, little corpses,
> Froth, snowy white, and bubbles. . . .

And more terrible still, but as it were on the other side of the synecdoche, is the catalogue of the Civil War dead in *Specimen Days*:

> The dead in this war—there they lie, strewing the fields and woods and valleys and battle-fields of the south . . . Gettysburgh, the West, Southwest—Vicksburgh—Chattanooga—the trenches of Petersburgh—the numberless battles, camps, hospitals everywhere—the crop reap'd by the mighty reapers, typhoid, dysentery, inflammations—and blackest and loathesomest of all, the dead and living burial-pits, the prison-pens of Andersonville, Salisbury, Belle-Isle, &c., (not Dante's pictured hell and all its woes, its degradations, filthy torments, excell'd those prisons)—the dead, the dead, the dead —*our* dead—or South or North, ours all, (all, all, all, finally dear to me)—

When metonymy and synecdoche fail Whitman, he experiences it in the physical world—the dead and dying strewn about him in the Civil War, signifying disintegration of the union and of the nation, and his own body failing him after the paralytic stroke. But Whitman found a wonderfully symbolic way to heal this latter division, a division within his body and between his body and the circumambient universe. He set about restoring health and wholeness through intimate absorption of and in the natural, physical world: at Timberlake he wrestled trees and found potency flowing from the trees into himself; another day he experienced much the same thing by stripping naked and taking a mud bath in "a particularly secluded little dell" where he alternated using a stiff brush to rasp "arms, breast, sides, till they turn'd scarlet," with bathing and "stepping about barefooted every few minutes now and then in some neighboring black ooze, for unctuous mud-bath to my feet" (*Walt Whitman: Poetry and Prose*, 806–7). Of one of his favorite trees — "a fine yellow poplar, quite straight, perhaps 90 feet high, and four thick at the butt" — Whitman exclaims, "How strong, vital, enduring! how dumbly eloquent! What suggestions of imperturbability and *being*, as against the human trait of mere *seeming*. Then the qualities, almost emotional, palpably artistic, heroic, of a tree; so innocent and harmless, yet so savage. It *is*, yet says nothing" (pp. 789–90). How many times have we heard that of a poem — that it should not mean but be? Whitman's trees possess that kind of presence naturally. The effect of wrestling with a tree — this time "a tough oak sapling thick as my wrist, twelve feet high" — Whitman describes thus: "After I wrestle with the tree awhile, I can feel its young sap and virtue welling up out of the ground and tingling through me from crown to toe, like health's wine" (p. 800) — as if the sap were a secular divine presence. Of the scene of his mud-bathing and tree-wrestling Whitman writes, "How it is I know not, but I often realize a *presence* here — in clear moods I am certain of it" (p. 809; my emphasis). At Timberlake it was, for Whitman, no trope to speak of a present presence. In clear moods he was certain of it.

Already in 1864, when he was only twenty years old, two years

before he was received into the Catholic church by John Henry
Newman and four years before he entered the Jesuit Novitiate,
Gerard Hopkins was writing from Oxford to Ernest Coleridge, a
former schoolmate of his at Highgate School, "Beware of doing
what I once thought I could do, *adopt an enlightened Christianity*,
I may say, horrible as it is, *be a credit to religion*. This fatal state
of mind leads to infidelity, if consistently and logically developed.
The great aid to belief and object of belief is the doctrine of the
Real Presence in the Blessed Sacrament of the Altar. Religion
without that is sombre, dangerous, illogical, with that it is—not to
speak of its grand consistency and certainty—*loveable*. Hold that
and you will gain all Catholic truth" (*Further Letters of GMH*, pp.
16–17). And some eighteen years later, writing to Robert Bridges,
Hopkins reaffirmed his sense of the ultimate importance of the
doctrine of the Real Presence: "Corpus Xti differs from all other
feasts in this, that its reason and occasion is present. The first
Christmas Day, the first Palm Sunday, Holy Thursday 'in Caena
Domini,' Easter, Whitsunday, and so on were to those who took
part in them festivities *de praesenti*, but now, to us, they are anni-
versaries and commemorations only. But Corpus Christi is the
feast of the Real Presence; therefore it is the most purely joyous
of solemnities" (*Letters to RB*, p. 149). It would be no exaggera-
tion to say that the essentially metaphoric doctrine of the Real
Presence—that is, that the body and blood of Christ are really but
invisibly present in the elements of the Eucharist—was the heart
and soul of Hopkins's religious belief and his poetic practice, and
further, that fear of its loss, fear of his own inability to experience
the Real Presence, and fear that he might violate that presence by
too great an attraction to things merely present without sufficient
regard for their presence was the greatest fear and torment of his
life. Emily Dickinson might take a kind of grisly delight in dis-
covering that the ultimate presence is really absence and so, by
way of metaphor, establishing an absent absence as the deepest
reality in certain of her poems; and Walt Whitman, especially in

the early poems, before the horrors of the Civil War and before his crippling stroke, might delight in the sheer physical, bodily presentness of things to that degree that his delight seemed to establish a present presence as the deepest reality; but Hopkins would have found either of these visions, representing respectively the dangers of metaphor and the dangers of metonymy, simply intolerable.

Whitman could write, in "I Sing the Body Electric,"

> I have perceiv'd that to be with those I like is enough,
> To stop in company with the rest at evening is enough,
> To be surrounded by beautiful, curious, breathing, laughing
>   flesh is enough,
> To pass among them or touch any one, or rest my arm ever so
>   lightly round his or her neck for a moment, what is this
>   then?
> I do not ask any more delight, I swim in it as in a sea.

As in his reconstitutive activities at Timberlake, Whitman could wrestle, wallow, revel, and swim in the presentness of things and thereby experience in them a presence. And he does, for example in the famous scene of twenty-eight bathers plus one in "Song of Myself," where the twenty-ninth bather may be intended to be the woman who comes to watch the twenty-eight young men and in imagination jumps in with them — but every reader feels, I think, that it is not some imaginary woman but the voyeuristic Whitman who is really gambolling with the young men in the water:

> The beards of the young men glisten'd with wet, it ran from
>   their long hair,
> Little streams pass'd all over their bodies.
>
> An unseen hand also pass'd over their bodies,
> It descended tremblingly from their temples and ribs.
>
> The young men float on their backs, their white bellies bulge
>   to the sun, they do not ask who seizes fast to them,

> They do not know who puffs and declines with pendant and
>   bending arch,
> They do not think whom they souse with spray.

Hopkins, too, loved the water and swimming, and he was—at least
as he felt—far too inclined to be attracted by the physical beauty
of boys and young men, but he had always to ask himself, as he
does in the title of one poem, "To What Serves Mortal Beauty?"
and his answer was that it did not simply serve itself, it was never
enough in itself, but on the contrary was highly, highly dangerous
taken in and for itself with nothing more to justify our attraction
to it. He could go so far in a Whitmanesque direction, however,
as to write more than forty lines of sheer delight in watching boys
bathing before remembering himself and pulling up short to turn
it into an arid allegory about marriage in the poem titled "Epithalamion." Even in the scene as he describes it, and much more
in the boys' bodies when they come on the scene, one can feel the
full potential of the Whitmanian Old Adam in Hopkins:

> Hark, hearer, hear what I do; lend a thought now, make believe
> We are leaf-whelmed somewhere with the hood
> Of some branchy bunchy bushybowered wood,
> Southern dean or Lancashire clough or Devon cleave,
> That leans along the loins of hills, where a candycoloured,
>   where a gluegold-brown
> Marbled river, boisterously beautiful, between
> Roots and rocks is danced and dandled, all in froth and
>   waterblowballs, down.

Into this scene of alliterative, natural ecstasy comes "the riot of a
rout / Of . . . boys from the town / Bathing" and then there arrives
"a listless stranger," unnamed but I think any reader understands
his name to be the same as the author of the poem:

> By there comes a listless stranger: beckoned by the noise
> He drops towards the river: unseen

Sees the bevy of them, how the boys
With dare and with downdolfinry and bellbright bodies
    huddling out,
Are earthworld, airworld, waterworld thorough hurled, all by
    turn and turn about.

"Unseen Sees"—how very like Whitman that is, forever gazing
and gazing, and how like Whitman too the unmoralized "bellbright bodies huddling out." Entirely captivated by the scene, the
listless stranger feels he, too, must get in the swim, if not actually
with the boys then close by:

This garland of their gambol flashes in his breast
Into such a sudden zest
Of summertime joys
That he hies to a pool neighbouring; sees it is the best
There; sweetest, freshest, shadowiest;
Fairyland; silk-beech, scrolled ash, packed sycamore, wild
    wychelm, hornbeam fretty overstood
By. . . .
        Here he feasts: lovely all is! No more: off with—down he
    dings
His bleached both and woolwoven wear:
Careless these in coloured wisp
All lie tumbled-to; then with loop-locks
Forward falling, forehead frowning, lips crisp
Over fingerteasing task, his twiny boots
Fast he opens, last he off wrings
Till walk the world he can with bare his feet. . . .

The eager excitement to get out of the clothes and the trembling
impatience over the "fingerteasing task" of getting the boots off
remind one of the unseen hand passing over the young men's
bodies and descending "tremblingly over their temples and ribs"
in Whitman's poem. But after allowing the now no longer listless

stranger to frolic in the pool as "the water warbles over" him with "glassy grassy quicksilvery shives and shoots / And with heaven fallen freshness down from moorland" brimming, Hopkins calls a sudden halt: Here "we leave him" to produce a dry-as-dust allegory, attempting to drag a spiritual meaning by main force into all this unmeaning bliss. The effort, as one might expect, proved futile and Hopkins left the poem a fragment, unfinished. Whether he consciously identified what he had been up to in the poem as Whitmanesque in what Hopkins would have had to think was the bad sense no one can say, but it seems to me certain that he dropped the poem so quickly because he recognized that it was not the Real Presence he was seeing in those "bellbright bodies," and that "all this juice and all this joy" (as he terms it in the poem "Spring") was a matter for him not of an absent presence but much more of a present absence.

It was not always so with Hopkins—it was sometimes worse, as in the late "terrible sonnets" or "sonnets of desolation" where he experienced both a present absence and an absent absence; and it was sometimes much better, as in the ten or twelve poems that followed the great breakthrough of "The Wreck of the Deutschland," where the Real Presence, though invisible and necessarily absent in itself, is really and richly present in the things of nature and even, in "As kingfishers catch fire," in the faces of men:

> For Christ plays in ten thousand places,
> Lovely in limbs, and lovely in eyes not his
> To the Father through the features of men's faces.

Before proceeding to the great but harrowing late sonnets we might pause over some of the early poems where the metaphoric rendering of an absent presence is so strikingly and joyously successful. "The world is charged with the grandeur of God," the first line of "God's Grandeur," is a characteristic expression of Hopkins's sense of unfailing spiritual presence in the early poems. All of creation is energized as with an electrical charge that is

none of humankind's doing though it is there as pulse and impulse for humans too if they do not refuse (or defuse) it. Hopkins
developed the same idea in some spiritual notes written some four
years after "God's Grandeur": "All things therefore are charged
with love, are charged with God and if we know how to touch
them give off sparks and take fire, yield drops and flow, ring and
tell of him" (*The Sermons and Devotional Writings of GMH*, p. 195).
It is a sense of the ubiquity and unfailingness of God's presence,
in spite of the perversity of the human will, that animates these
early poems as in the sestet of "God's Grandeur":

> And, for all this, nature is never spent;
>   There lives the dearest freshness deep down things;
> And though the last lights off the black West went
>   Oh, morning, at the brown brink eastwards, springs —
> Because the Holy Ghost over the bent
>   World broods with warm breast and with ah! bright wings.

In the single word "bent" and in the subtle interplay of *b*'s and
w's in these last lines Hopkins suggests the charged and fecund
richness of nature, as a result of God's presence, that is the poem's
theme. The way in which Hopkins bends the word "bent" over the
enjambed line, pointing simultaneously to the world as morally
bent, to the physical bend of the earth's curvature, and to the
Holy Ghost's couvadelike bending in concern over the human
world; the double sense of "broods" in the last line as both in-
cubating and worrying over; and the *w/b*'s of "World broods"
and "warm breast" that are chiasmatically reversed in the *b/w*
of "bright wings" after the release of wonderment in "ah!" — in
all these Hopkins is technically imitating the charged richness of
God's presence throughout creation.

No doubt Hopkins's finest achievement in this way of figur-
ing Christ's presence in the world under the guise of a natural
creature is "The Windhover" (Hopkins himself called it "the best
thing I ever wrote" [*Letters to RB*, p. 85]). The metaphorical sub-

stitution that says that the observable attributes of the falcon "a billion times told lovelier" = the attributes of Christ = the essential nature of Christ as incarnate and discarnate God holds more firmly in "The Windhover" than in any other of Hopkins's poems, which is to say that the invisible presence of Christ is realized more successfully, is more completely visualized and made more visualizable, in the flight of the falcon than anywhere else in Hopkins. The success of the poem depends first of all on the complete realization and visualization of the near term of the metaphor, the falcon and its flight, and second on the effectiveness of the transfer of the falcon's attributes to the far term of the metaphor, the essential nature of Christ. To put it in other words, I believe that there is in the octet of the poem a metonymic identification of the poet with something present and contiguous in nature — "My heart in hiding / Stirred for a bird, — the achieve of, the mastery of the thing" — and this metonymic identification of the octet is transformed in the sestet of the poem into a metaphoric identification with something not of the natural and visible world, the essence of Christ's life in and out of time.[10] Here is the poem, which Hopkins dedicated "to Christ our Lord":

> I caught this morning morning's minion, king-
>> dom of daylight's dauphin, dapple-dawn-drawn Falcon, in
>>> his riding
> Of the rolling level underneath him steady air, and striding
> High there, how he rung upon the rein of a wimpling wing
> In his ecstacy! then off, off forth on swing,
>> As a skate's heel sweeps smooth on a bow-bend: the hurl
>>> and gliding
> Rebuffed the big wind. My heart in hiding
> Stirred for a bird, — the achieve of, the mastery of the thing!
>
> Brute beauty and valour and act, oh, air, pride, plume, here
>> Buckle! AND the fire that breaks from thee then, a billion
> Times told lovelier, more dangerous, O my chevalier!

No wonder of it: sheer plod makes plough down sillion
Shine, and blue-bleak embers, ah my dear,
   Fall, gall themselves, and gash gold-vermilion.

One sees all of Hopkins's technical resources on fullest display here: his sprung rhythm is extraordinarily effective in capturing the bird's flight; the rhyme, both end rhyme and internal rhyme, and the assonance and alliteration are themselves instances of the "beauty and valour and act" that they both celebrate and imitate; and the sonnet form, about which Hopkins held ideas that were virtually mystical,[11] is handled perfectly, with great skill and to very telling effect. "What you look hard at seems to look hard at you," Hopkins once noted in his journal (*Journals and Papers*, p. 204), and it is a very active process that establishes the metonymies of the octet of the poem: "I *caught* this morning. . . ." The bird, its activity and its attributes, are fully present in the first eight lines of the poem, but were this all — were Hopkins not to go on to make the metaphoric transfer and substitution in the sestet — then, according to his own understanding, he would have accomplished no more than the sort of failed fragment, beautiful perhaps but meaningless, that he produced in "Epithalamion." It is in the word that has become a famous crux in the poem — "Buckle" — that the metaphoric transfer occurs. "Buckle," as commentators have pointed out, has several possible meanings, some of them apparently contradictory, and most or all of those meanings seem to me active at this point in the poem. There is first the physical action of the bird, carried over from the octet, soaring and gliding and now, in the most daring, the most beautiful of his movements, folding and buckling his wings to plummet downward in free fall at tremendous speed. In this sense of "buckle," the "chevalier" of Hopkins's apostrophe in line 11 remains the falcon whose buckling and diving action is "a billion times told lovelier, more dangerous" than the performance of the octet. But buckle may also mean to crumple or to give way, and it must

be something other and much more than a bird that is capable
of producing infinitely greater, more dangerous beauty than the
bird's beauty by crumpling and giving way. "O my chevalier,"
then, while continuing to reach back to the falcon, now reaches
forward to Christ, even in the rhymes that Hopkins deploys so
effectively—"here," "chevalier," and "dear." It is "here" that all is
buckled into one metaphor, the "chevalier" referring to both the
falcon and Christ; and when "O my chevalier" finds its perfect
rhyme and symmetrical partner in "ah my dear," the transfer is
made entirely to Christ, for I think there can be no doubt but that
in "ah my dear" Hopkins is deliberately echoing George Herbert,
his favorite poet in the English tradition, who, in "Love (III),"
addresses Christ in precisely the same phrase: "Ah, my dear, I cannot look on thee." In the final tercet, the terms that in the octet
were entirely physical and in the first tercet of the sestet were
half-physical, half-spiritual, are now entirely moral and spiritual,
thoroughly transformed by the power of metaphor. In the end
buckling means crumpling, falling, giving way, and it also means
buckling to a task, putting one's hand to the plough, as the priest
must do in imitation of Christ's life—"sheer plod makes plough
down sillion / Shine"—with both actions, crumpling and taking
on an inglorious task, seen as acts of sacrifice deliberately chosen:
sacrifice of great physical beauty to gain a moral, spiritual beauty
that is "a billion times told lovelier." The description of Christ's
surpassing physical beauty that Hopkins gave in a sermon to his
congregation at Bedford Leigh (*Sermons and Devotional Writings*,
p. 35) and his remark in a letter to Richard Watson Dixon that
Christ "was doomed to succeed by failure" (p. 138) are both of
them relevant here. "The Windhover" is one of those poems that
seem almost miraculous in coming so far from the beginning of
the poem that one cannot see how it has been done—how Hopkins can get from "I caught this morning morning's minion" to
"blue bleak embers, ah my dear / Fall, gall themselves, and gash
gold-vermilion"; and yet the end of the poem is so tightly bound

through created meaning to the beginning that, after the fact, it appears almost inevitable.

"The Windhover," however, was written in the wonderful period that Hopkins spent at St. Beuno's in Wales, and while he later wrote some poems of unquestioned excellence he never again married so successfully the strengths of metonymy and metaphor. Moreover, when he did have success with one or the other or both kinds of tropes it was most often to express feelings of misery and failure, as if something had gone wrong with the troping of his mind and spirit and the "ductile anchor" that Whitman was sure would hold somewhere never would do that for Hopkins. Whitman could write with confidence in "Song of Myself" that grass "is the handkerchief of the Lord, / A scented gift and remembrancer designedly dropt[12] / Bearing the owner's name someway in the corners" (section 6) and he could declare,

I hear and behold God in every object. . . ,
I see something of God each hour of the twenty-four, and
    each moment then,
In the faces of men and women I see God, and in my own face
    in the glass,[13]
I find letters from God dropt in the street, and every one is
    sign'd by God's name . . .

(section 48)

but Hopkins felt no such assurance. In the late poems he for the most part not only fails to "find letters from God dropt in the street," but also feels that his own letters to that same correspondent have dropped into a void or into some black hole in the universe[14] as in the poem that begins "I wake and feel the fell of dark, not day":

And my lament
Is cries countless, cries like dead letters sent
To dearest him that lives alas! away.

Hopkins's metaphors discover no presence on the other side, and they are, as it were, returned to him stamped "Addressee Unknown." I can think of no more desperate expression of what I have called present absence than this. I say "present absence" rather than "absent absence" because Hopkins, in this and the other "sonnets of desolation," was all too present to himself—miserably present—but there was no presence in that presentness:

> I am gall, I am heartburn. God's most deep decree
> Bitter would have me taste: my taste was me;
> Bones built in me, flesh filled, blood brimmed the curse.
>
> Selfyeast of spirit a dull dough sours. I see
> The lost are like this, and their scourge to be
> As I am mine, their sweating selves; but worse.

This sense of imprisonment in the body or of the body's betrayal and failure, reflected in failure and absence in the body of the world, is echoed in two journal entries in which Hopkins describes, respectively, the aftereffects of a nightmare and the experience of being unwell:

> I thought something or someone leapt onto me and held me quite fast: this I think woke me. . . . This first start is . . . a nervous collapse. . . . I had lost all muscular stress. . . . The feeling is terrible: the body no longer swayed as a piece by the nervous and muscular instress seems to fall in and hang like a dead weight on the chest. . . . It made me think that this was how the souls in hell would be imprisoned in their bodies . . . (*Journals and Papers*, p. 238).

> But we hurried too fast and it knocked me up. We went to the College, the seminary being wanted for the secular priests' retreat: almost no gas, for the retorts are being mended; therefore candles in bottles, things not ready, darkness and despair. In fact being unwell I was quite downcast: nature in

all her parcels and faculties gaped and fell apart, *fatiscebat*, like
a clod cleaving and holding only by strings of root (*Journals
and Papers*, p. 236).

But these two descriptions of metonymic failure—one of the body
as a prison, the other of correspondent collapses in the body and
in nature—are concerned with abnormal conditions of nightmare
and sickness. The sonnets of desolation seem to record Hopkins's
experience and his vision of what was apparently the normal condition for him in the last three or four years of his life.

I have been speaking of failure but I do not want to be understood to mean that the late poems themselves are failures; on the
contrary, as poetry they are very powerful and as grand in their
achievements as "The Windhover" or "God's Grandeur" or "The
Wreck of the Deutschland." But the world discovered by his metonymies and metaphors had to be, for someone of Hopkins's
beliefs, truly terrifying. "Spelt from Sibyl's Leaves" is, I think,
one of Hopkins's finest poems, a poem of great aural beauty but
depicting a world of ultimate bleakness, and it seems to me the
most profoundly pessimistic thing, bordering even on nihilism,[15]
that Hopkins ever wrote—which is saying a lot, since Hopkins
concludes "No worst" with these lines: "Here! creep, / Wretch,
under a comfort serves in a whirlwind: all / Life death does end
and each day dies with sleep." This is a comfort? Nietzsche (who
said, "The thought of suicide is a great consolation: by means of
it one gets successfully through many a bad night") might have
found it so and perhaps Emily Dickinson, but few of the rest of us.
Things are even worse, however, in "Spelt from Sibyl's Leaves."
As "[e]vening strains to be time's vast, womb-of-all, home-of-
all, hearse-of-all night," Hopkins imagines apocalyptic darkness
come to end everything, himself and the world alike. It is difficult
to recall in reading the poem that Hopkins is, at one level, only
describing the coming of night, for the obliteration of beauty,
of peace, of very being is so total; but then night is the spiri-

tual time of all the sonnets of desolation, when Hopkins wakes
and feels "the fell of dark, not day," when a predatory beast lays
"a lionlimb against" him and scans "with darksome devouring
eyes" his bruised bones, and when he is forced to cry out, "O the
mind, mind has mountains; cliffs of fall / Frightful, sheer, no-
man-fathomed." This is the time of the dark night of the soul, and
in "Spelt from Sibyl's Leaves" there is no suggestion that there
will be any issuing from it. In "God's Grandeur," "though the last
lights off the black West went / Oh, morning, at the brown brink
eastwards, springs," but not here, not in the world of "Sibyl's
Leaves":

> For earth her being has unbound; her dapple is at
>   end, as-
> Tray or aswarm, all throughther, in throngs; self in self steeped
>   and pashed — quite
> Disremembering, dismembering all now. Heart, you round me
>   right
> With: Our evening is over us; our night whelms, whelms, and
>   will end us.

There are lessons to be drawn from this — some very stark and
grim moral lessons — but no cheer is offered and no comfort either.
Though the language is a good deal more intense and the movement of the verse is quite different, the mood of the end of the
poem reminds one of Whitman's mood of dark pessimism in "As
I Ebb'd with the Ocean of Life":

> Let life, waned, ah let life wind
> Off her once skeined stained veined variety upon, all on two
>   spools; part, pen, pack
> Now her all in two flocks, two folds — black, white; right,
>   wrong; reckon but, reck but, mind
> But these two; ware of a world where but these two tell, each
>   off the other; of a rack

Where, selfwrung, selfstrung, sheathe- and shelterless,
   thoughts against thoughts in groans grind.

The imperative of "let life wind / Off her once skeined stained veined variety upon, all on two spools" enjoins the individual to turn away from or to sacrifice the world of natural beauty celebrated in such earlier poems as "Spring," "Hurrahing in Harvest," "Pied Beauty," and "Inversnaid" in favor of a world where one can only choose, and must choose, between stark moral opposites, "black, white; right, wrong"; but the poem offers little or nothing in return for this sacrifice: there is no gold-vermilion at the end of "Sibyl's Leaves" as there is at the end of "The Windhover." It may be that what Hopkins is describing in the last lines is the Hell to which the sinful soul will descend after death, there to suffer the consequences of the moral choices made and not made in this life, but the lines seem to me to refer first of all and most naturally not to an afterworld but to the present world devoid of its "once skeined stained veined variety" — which I suppose would be a kind of hell after all. It was, I think without question, the world Hopkins lived in at the time of the poem.

It is a mark of Hopkins's accomplishment that he could turn the material of his sad last years into poems possessed of the power and pathos of the late works. Even more remarkable, perhaps, is what he does in two of his very last poems, "Justus quidem tu es, Domine" and "To R. B.," each of them a great poem consisting essentially and paradoxically of a lament and explanation for his inability to write a poem. In the first poem even as he laments the failure of the metonymy between his own creativity and natural fecundity he reestablishes the metonymy:

See, banks and brakes
Now, leavèd how thick! lacèd they are again
With fretty chervil, look, and fresh wind shakes

Them; birds build — but not I build; no, but strain

> Time's eunuch, and not breed one work that wakes.
> Mine, O thou lord of life, send my roots rain.

There is a deep pathos in these last lines that does not, however, yield to sentimentality, and out of his straining as "Time's
eunuch," out of his inability to "breed one work that wakes,"
Hopkins brings forth just such a work quick with life. Likewise, a
crucial line — and the whole poem really — of "To R. B." belies the
presented subject, which is the poet's infertility. Hopkins employs
an extraordinarily interesting metaphor of sexual intercourse and
conception to develop this subject, a metaphor which might be
expressed in the following equation: as, in intercourse, the male
member is to the woman's womb, so, in poetry, inspiration ("the
strong / Spur, live and lancing like the blowpipe flame") is to the
mind of the poet.

> The fine delight that fathers thought; the strong
> Spur, live and lancing like the blowpipe flame,
> Breathes once and, quenched faster than it came,
> Leaves yet the mind a mother of immortal song.
>
> Nine months she then, nay years, nine years she long
> Within her wears, bears, cares and combs the same:
> The widow of an insight lost she lives, with aim
> Now known and hand at work now never wrong.
>
> Sweet fire the sire of muse, my soul needs this;
> I want the one rapture of an inspiration.
> O then if in my lagging lines you miss
>
> The roll, the rise, the carol, the creation,
> My winter world, that scarcely breathes that bliss
> Now, yields you, with some sighs, our explanation.

The twin acts of impregnation and gestation presented in the
octet are, according to Hopkins, no longer possible to him because
the "strong spur" is missing, leaving the mind an unimpregnated

and empty womb. But the very lines of the sestet that explain his nonfecundity belie it: "O then if in my lagging lines you miss / The roll, the rise, the carol, the creation. . . ." The pregnancy that Hopkins says is not to be found in his lines is in fact there in the swelling-out sound of "the roll, the rise, the carol, the creation," which imitates and establishes the pregnant fertility of the poem itself.

By their figures ye shall know them. Dickinson, Whitman, Hopkins—all poets really—are as distinctive, as marked off, by the figures and tropes they employ as by those rhythms that seem a correlation of their individual being. What Dickinson did with metaphor, Whitman with metonymy and synecdoche, and Hopkins now with one, now with another, sometimes with both or all, was to expand, each in her/his special way, the expressive powers of language and to leave a legacy to other poets to expand those powers in the same way and beyond. What they did, in other words, each of them, was to push figurative language to boundaries and frontiers, to extremes that it had not known before and would not have known without them. But distinctiveness and extremes are, in a way, the subject of my next lecture, so I will leave it there for now.

CHAPTER THREE

Making Strange

A Jesuit priest who spent his noviceship at Stonyhurst some forty years or more after Hopkins was there to do his three years of philosophy tells of asking an old lay brother for anything he might remember about Hopkins. "One of Hopkins's special delights, said the brother, was the path from the Seminary to the College. After a shower, he would run and crouch down to gaze at the crushed quartz glittering as the sun came out again. 'Ay, a strange yoong man,' said the old brother, 'crouching down that gate to stare at some wet sand. A fair natural 'e seemed to us, that Mr. 'opkins'" (*Journals and Papers*, p. 408). The old lay brother and his bemused companions were wrong about Hopkins being a natural—i.e., someone born without a normal share of intelligence and understanding—but that he was "a strange yoong man" is probably accurate enough. Not stranger than Emily Dickinson or Walt Whitman however. Responding to T. W. Higginson's request for a picture of herself, Dickinson wrote, "I had no portrait, now, but am small, like the Wren, and my Hair is bold, like the Chestnut Bur—and my eyes, like the Sherry in the Glass, that the Guest leaves— . . . Myself the only Kangaroo among the Beauty, Sir, if you please, it afflicts me, and I thought that instruction would take it away" (*Letters*, #268). Whitman, on the other hand, was not afflicted by his strangeness or his standing out awkwardly, Kangaroolike "among the Beauty." In one of the anonymous reviews of *Leaves of Grass* that he awarded himself, Whitman, after quoting from "Song of Myself" ("I am the poet of the Body and

I am the poet of the Soul," etc.), goes on to exclaim, "It is indeed a strange voice! Critics and lovers and readers of poetry as hitherto written, may well be excused the chilly and unpleasant shudders which will assuredly run through them, to their very blood and bones, when they first read Walt Whitman's poems. If this is poetry, where must its foregoers stand?" (*In Re Walt Whitman*, pp. 30–31). This originality and strangeness of Whitman the man and the poet could, of course, be seen in another light, as is apparent in the comment of a different, less intimately connected reviewer of the first edition of *Leaves of Grass*. "That he was one of the roughs," Charles Eliot Norton wrote of the poet of *Leaves of Grass*, "was . . . tolerably plain; but that he was a kosmos was a piece of news we were hardly prepared for."[1] The strangeness I want to think about, however, is not the strangeness of Hopkins crouching in the garden to stare at some pieces of quartz, and not the strangeness of Dickinson's self-description nor her feeling of being different from those around her, nor yet the strangeness of one of the roughs also proclaiming himself a kosmos, but rather the strangeness that is to be found *in their poetry* and, I will argue, in all writing to which we grant the high name of poetry. It is a question not of *being* strange but of *making* strange, although in the end the two may come to the same thing since the great poets do see differently from the rest of us: they see farther and deeper into language and the human condition, and their vision will always, necessarily seem strange as coming from the extreme bounds — and beyond — of human experience and expression.

"No doubt my poetry errs on the side of oddness," Hopkins wrote to Robert Bridges. "I hope in time to have a more balanced and Miltonic style. [This Hopkins never achieved, and one wonders if it was really a deep desire on his part.] But as air, melody, is what strikes me most of all in music and design in painting, so design, pattern or what I am in the habit of calling 'inscape' is what I above all aim at in poetry. Now it is the virtue of design, pattern, or inscape to be distinctive and it is the vice of distinctiveness to become queer. This vice I cannot have escaped" (*Letters to RB*, p. 66). Distinctiveness and queerness are the opposite sides of the coin of strangeness, and that coin was in Hopkins's eyes — and I would think in Dickinson's too — of such value that he would accept the charge of queerness as simply the cost of achieving in-scape and distinctiveness. Turn this just a bit further, however, and it becomes apparent that what Hopkins and Dickinson were ultimately aiming at, with distinctiveness, queerness, and strange-ness halfway houses on the way there, was what we can only call — and in the highest sense — mystery. "You do not mean by mys-tery what a Catholic does," Hopkins wrote to Bridges. "You mean an interesting uncertainty: the uncertainty ceasing interest ceases also. This happens in some things; to you in religion. But a Catho-lic by mystery means an incomprehensible certainty" (*Letters to RB*, p. 187). This sense of mystery invests Hopkins's poetry with a special weightedness but also, in the late poetry, with a special anguish when he felt himself cut off from it. Cast in secular and social terms, the classic expression of strangeness as the principle of poetry-making is no doubt Dickinson's poem #435:

> Much Madness is divinest Sense —
> To a discerning Eye —
> Much Sense — the starkest Madness —
> 'Tis the Majority
> In this, as All, prevail —
> Assent — and you are sane —
> Demur — you're straightway dangerous —
> And handled with a Chain —

In the more unfettered style of "Song of Myself" distinctiveness sounds like this: "Unscrew the locks from the doors! / Unscrew the doors themselves from their jambs!" — for "Walt Whitman, a kosmos, of Manhattan the son" is at hand, or if not at hand then overhead: "I too am not a bit tamed, I too am untranslatable, / I sound my barbaric yawp over the roofs of the world."

"As kingfishers catch fire, dragonflies draw flame," and Walt Whitmans sound their barbaric yawp—this, in effect, is the theme both stated and enacted in Hopkins's poem:

As kingfishers catch fire, dragonflies draw flame;
   As tumbled over rim in roundy wells
   Stones ring; like each tucked string tells, each hung bell's
Bow swung finds tongue to fling out broad its name;
Each mortal thing does one thing and the same:
   Deals out that being indoors each one dwells;
   Selves—goes its self; *myself* it speaks and spells,
Crying *What I do is me: for that I came*.[2]

To transform the noun "self" into a verb, "to selve"—it's not in my dictionary anyway—is to embody linguistically that distinctiveness that the line is about. In and through the poem Hopkins "selves" himself, speaks and spells himself, "crying *What I do is me: for that I came*." Just so, "Song of Myself" selves Walt Whitman; in the "Song" Whitman "finds tongue to fling out broad [his] name." And does not Dickinson's poem #613 constitute a particularized selving for her even as it declares that that is what poetry is supremely for—a means to selving for the individual?

They shut me up in Prose—
As when a little Girl
They put me in the Closet—
Because they liked me "still"—

Still! Could themself have peeped—
And seen my Brain—go round—
They might as wise have lodged a Bird
For Treason—in the Pound—

Himself has but to will
And easy as a Star
Abolish his Captivity—
And laugh—No more have I—

They—the forces arrayed against her as noisy little girl and as adult poet—are no more going to keep Emily Dickinson "still," they are no more going to prevent her dealing "out that being indoors each one dwells," than they are going to silence Whitman's "barbaric yawp" or Hopkins's claim that, by virtue of Christ's Incarnation, Crucifixion, and Resurrection,

> In a flash, at a trumpet crash,
> I am all at once what Christ is, since he was what I am, and
> This Jack, joke, poor potsherd, patch, matchwood, immortal
> diamond,
> Is immortal diamond.
> ("That Nature is a Heraclitean Fire and of the comfort of the
> Resurrection")

For Hopkins (but not for Dickinson or Whitman), this is the ultimate significance of selving—that as Christ was the most highly individuated, the most intensely inscaped, the most thoroughly distinctive of beings, so each individual, by the act of selving, by going itself, by speaking and spelling "*myself*," is imitating Christ in the world. Thus the sestet of "As kingfishers catch fire":

> I say more: the just man justices;
> Keeps grace: that keeps all his goings graces;
> Acts in God's eye what in God's eye he is—
> Christ. For Christ plays in ten thousand places,
> Lovely in limbs, and lovely in eyes not his
> To the Father through the features of men's faces.

This is the ultimate source and justification for selving, according to Hopkins, but he was also capable of seeing selving as a principle of composition in a nontheological context as in "Henry Purcell," where it is the "arch-especial" spirit of Purcell, translated into the forms of music, that affects Hopkins so strongly and draws him to Purcell: "It is the forgèd feature finds me; it is the rehearsal / Of own, of abrupt self there so thrusts on, so throngs the ear." In this poem, as in others on similar subjects, Hopkins is as distinctively Hopkins, is as "arch-especial a spirit" in poetic ways, as Purcell is Purcell in musical ways. In fact, Hopkins is so distinctively himself in the first quatrain —

> Have fair fallen, O fair, fair have fallen, so dear
> To me, so arch-especial a spirit as heaves in Henry Purcell,
> An age is now since passed, since parted; with the reversal
> Of the outward sentence low lays him, listed to a heresy,
> here —

that he had to spend the better part of three longish letters to Robert Bridges explaining how to construe the grammar and what the lines were to mean. Although the meaning was put very simply in the first letter — "I hope Purcell is not damned for being a Protestant, because I love his genius." — it was not until the third letter that the grammar of "Have fair fallen" was satisfactorily explained: "This is a terrible business about my sonnet 'Have fair fallen,' for I find that I still 'make myself misunderstood.' *Have* is not a plural at all, far from it. It is the singular imperative (or optative if you like) of the past, a thing possible and actual both in logic and grammar, but naturally a rare one" (*Letters to RB*, pp. 170, 174). Whether responsibility for misunderstanding lay more with Bridges or with Hopkins there can be no doubt that the singularity of Hopkins's expression, designed to reflect the singularity of Purcell's music, played its part in the difficulty.

The quality of strangeness can, of course, be inflected in many different ways. To choose only the most obvious terms of inflection, it can be viewed as eccentricity, queerness, madness, distinctiveness, uniqueness, originality, unconventionality, peculiarity, oddness, singularity, quaintness — no doubt there are more synonyms; and we are all familiar with the notion that strangeness is the inevitable companion of what we were once taught to call genius. Einstein acted in strange ways, sticking out his tongue at photographers, forgetting to wear socks, etc., but then that was just a part of the package of being a genius. At its highest and most potent, however—and now I am thinking not of everyday notions of the queer, the peculiar, and the singular but of strangeness as it manifests itself in poetry—strangeness is not to be thought of as mere eccentricity or quaintness but rather as something that points to a mysteriousness or a mysterious something beyond our capacity for rational formulation but rich nevertheless in felt meaning. It is the very nature of mystery that it should strike us as being, in equal degrees, strange and meaningful. I think that it was something of this sort that T. S. Eliot had in mind when he praised the poetry of Walter de la Mare—poetry shot through with feeling for the strange and the uncanny—for its resourceful awareness of "the inexplicable mystery of sound." It is not sound alone, however, that, in the hands of the poet, may convey a sense of inexplicable mystery. Strangeness and its concomitant mysteriousness, as I have already implied, can be a matter of rhythmic peculiarity—for example, Dickinson's individual skewing of Common Meter to the point that it is scarcely recognizable: "Remorse is cureless—the Disease / Not even God—can heal— / For 'tis His institution—and / The Adequate of Hell—"; or it can be a distinctive way of troping, as in those metonymies and synecdoches of Whitman that present him as a "kosmos," both micro- and macro-. But strangeness and mystery can play themselves out at various other levels as well, in addition to the levels of sound, rhythm, and troping—at levels of vocabulary, syntax, form, theme, and vision—and it is these means of making strange that I want to consider for the remainder of this lecture. But I must point out that there is no way really to separate these various levels off from one another. It is one and the same strangeness in Hopkins's case, let us say, that manifests itself as peculiar rhythm and figurative language, as peculiar vocabulary, syntax, form, theme, and vision. "How all is one way wrought!" Hopkins exclaims in an unfinished and untitled poem, "How all things suit and sit!" And in poem #680 Dickinson writes to much the same effect:

Each Life Converges to some Centre —
Expressed — or still —
Exists in every Human Nature
A Goal —
Embodied scarcely to itself — it may be —
Too fair
For Credibility's presumption
To mar —

Adored with caution — as a Brittle Heaven —
To reach
Were hopeless, as the Rainbow's Raiment
To touch —

Taking our cue from Hopkins and Dickinson we might say that the ultimate source of the mystery and strangeness in any poem or body of poetry is perhaps to be sought in the strangeness of individual personality and the mystery of individual life.

Indeed, strangeness and mystery, or in his terms, oddness and inscape, were the twin principles of both Hopkins's poetics and his religious philosophy; and though she did not theorize about it as Hopkins did, one could well say that a sense of strangeness and mystery is responsible for much of the powerful affect of Dickinson's poetry. "No doubt my poetry errs on the side of oddness," as Hopkins put the matter to Bridges; but were it not for some telltale marks of diction and punctuation (i.e., a relatively prosaic diction and an absence of dashes) this could well have been from a letter of Emily Dickinson. Indeed, here is Dickinson to similar effect sending some poems to T. W. Higginson: "Are these more orderly? I thank you for the Truth — . . . . I think you called me 'Wayward.' Will you help me improve?" (*Letters*, #271). Hopkins was no more likely than Whitman to ask for help in improving and smoothing out the roughnesses of his poetry (see Whitman in one of his self-reviews: "Meanwhile a strange voice parts others aside and demands for its owner that position that is only allowed after the seal of many returning years has stamped with approving stamp the claims of the loftiest leading genius" [*In Re Walt Whitman*, p. 30]), but this temperamental difference apart—and it is difficult to say how sincere Dickinson was in requesting help or how much correction she would have accepted were it offered—they are all three very much at one on the principle of oddity in poetry.

The question of singularity is a complicated one, for we demand something of uniqueness in what we consider to be estimable poetry but if the singularity is too great the result is obscurity and incomprehension. The line between the kind of singularity that is to be admired and the eccentricity or obscurity that is to be avoided is a fine and wavering one, but it is a line that readers must draw—though of course they will differ on where to draw it—in Hopkins, in Dickinson, and in Whitman alike. "You give me a long jobation about eccentricities," Hopkins wrote to Bridges. "Alas, I have heard so much about and suffered so much for and in fact been so completely ruined for life by my alleged singularities that they are a sore subject" (*Letters to RB*, p. 126). Surely Dickinson must often have felt something of the same even though she professed herself ready to be corrected and made less "wayward" by Higginson. And Whitman drew a picture—though this was largely mythmaking—of blank incomprehension or scurrilous rejection by reviewers of what he was trying to accomplish, or had accomplished, in the 1855 *Leaves of Grass*. The consequence of what some took to be an excess of singularity in their poetry was that Dickinson and Hopkins were not published in anything approaching a full way until some thirty years after their deaths, and even then it was a good many more years before the poems were printed as Dickinson and Hopkins would have wished them to be. Whitman, of course, being Whitman, oversaw the printing, publishing, publicizing, distribution, and reviewing of his poetry, but this only reinforces the point, for had he not done all this

himself—had he not, in effect, been self-published—his poetry
too would have languished due to its singularity.[3] For all three of
them, and this must be true in some degree for all poets, the situation presented a sort of double bind: the kind of poetry they were
compelled to write was, like themselves, singular in the highest
degree, yet that very singularity, which made it the finest poetry
of its time, also made it unacceptable to general literary taste.
Hopkins spelled the dilemma out when he sent a copy of "That
Nature is a Heraclitean Fire and of the comfort of the Resurrection" to Robert Bridges: "I *must* read something of Greek and
Latin letters and lately I sent you a sonnet, on the Heraclitean
Fire, in which a great deal of early Greek philosophical thought
was distilled; but the liquor of the distillation did not taste very
Greek, did it? The effect of studying masterpieces is to make me
admire and do otherwise. So it must be on every original artist to
some degree, on me to a marked degree. Perhaps then more reading would only *refine my singularity*, which is not what you want"
(*Letters to RB*, p. 291; italics in the original). This inclination in
Hopkins to admire masterpieces and "do otherwise" was shared
by both Dickinson and Whitman, though the latter may sometimes have failed to admire very thoroughly before going on to do
otherwise. Dickinson wrote to Higginson of some poems she had
sent him, "I marked a line in One Verse—because I met it after I
made it—and never consciously touch a paint, mixed by another
person—" (*Letters*, #271). This may seem a little overfastidious,
to strike out a line already written after encountering something
similar, but heretofore unknown, in another poet; be that as it
may, however, this instinct never to repeat what is known already
to have been done is what makes Dickinson as a poet (and, one
might add, as a letter writer) so utterly different from any other
one can think of. And Whitman everywhere declares (as here in
"A Backward Glance O'er Travel'd Roads") that with American
democracy the time has "imperatively come" for "a readjustment
of the whole theory and nature of Poetry" (*Walt Whitman: Poetry*

and Prose, p. 662), a poetry that would have "*a Person*, a human being (myself, in the latter half of the Nineteenth Century, in America)" as its center and circumference. As Whitman himself said of the result of this "readjustment of the whole theory and nature of Poetry," "It is indeed a strange voice!"

"Making strange" in poetry involves not only consciously or unconsciously making individual strangenesses, choosing the odd word or the unusual image, but it also, and even more, means drawing on resources of the language that have been somehow neglected or lost, resources that were once available but that have become submerged in the unconscious of the language and that now, although still deeply a part of the language, appear strange, but charged with mysterious meaning, when brought back into consciousness. In a sense, this is equivalent to revivifying dead metaphors — i.e., metaphors that have become buried in the language — by pointing up the genesis and evolution of their metaphoric sense (as Hopkins does, for example, in giving a double punning meaning to "broods" in "God's Grandeur," referring both to the bird brooding over eggs and to the Holy Spirit brooding, like a parent, over a troubled world: the reader suddenly realizes that the bird literally brooding over her eggs is the source of the second, extended, metaphoric meaning of the word "brood"). Writers in English from other than the Anglo-American tradition — writers from Africa, India, the Caribbean, or even Welsh, Irish, and Scots writers — are forever giving a new charge or a new vitality to the language by recalling or rediscovering the elements that have been forgotten or half-forgotten by native speakers of English ("Standard English") whose only language it is and who thus are too familiar with it to see some of the possibilities buried in it. This serves to defamiliarize — to "estrange" or make strange — that which has become overfamiliar. In writing against the tradition to make strange, these writers in effect remake the tradition. Dickinson, Whitman, and Hopkins were of course within the

Anglo-American tradition so they hadn't this sort of outsider's insight into the possibilities of English, but Dickinson accomplished much the same sort of thing by, among other ways, adopting a little-girl persona, pretending to be approaching the language as someone absolutely fresh to it; Whitman did likewise with his New American persona and his claim that the American language was a new and different thing from the English language that had become tired and effete from centuries of use; and Hopkins worked his variation with a display of breathless eagerness before language and languages—English (including dialectal variations of Cumberland, Devonshire, Lancashire, Shropshire, and Yorkshire), German, French, Greek, Welsh—and by a return to etymological roots.

At the level of vocabulary, Hopkins, Dickinson, and Whitman shaped their distinctive languages most often not from words that were absolutely new but from words newly recovered from having been half-lost; from words freshly formed, according to regular principles of the language, out of roots and elements already present; from words in current use thrown into stunningly unusual contexts; and from foreign words and specialized or technical words used in a nontechnical passage of English. We can see Hopkins working in a couple of these ways in a relatively uncomplicated poem like "Pied Beauty" where the language praising all things "strange" is itself both strange and familiar, reflecting at one and the same time the mystery of natural beauty and its homeliness:

> Glory be to God for dappled things—
>   For skies of couple-colour as a brinded cow;
>   For rose-moles all in stipple upon trout that swim;
> Fresh-firecoal chestnut-falls; finches' wings;
>   Landscape plotted and pieced—fold, fallow, and plough;
>   And all trades, their gear and tackle and trim.

> All things counter, original, spare, strange;
> Whatever is fickle, freckled (who knows how?)
> With swift, slow; sweet, sour; adazzle, dim;
> He fathers-forth whose beauty is past change:
> Praise him.

There are an astonishing number of words in this short poem that bear looking at very closely: pied, dappled, couple-colour, brinded, rose-moles, stipple, fresh-firecoal, chestnut-falls, fold, fallow, plough, gear, tackle, trim, counter, spare, fickle, freckled, and fathers-forth—all these at a bare minimum, but they constitute pretty much the entire poem. It is a mark of Hopkins's genius that these words are all of them strange and not strange, "counter, original, spare," but, as the poem asks, "Who knows how?" "Pied" is not an uncommon word, but I imagine that most of us think of it only in conjunction with "Piper," and were it not for the Pied Piper one wonders if the word would still be current; in any case, to join "Pied" with "Beauty" is to give a wholly other sense to the word. Moreover, the dictionary gives another definition for "pied," a semitechnical definition reflecting Hopkins's love of "all trades, their gear and tackle and trim," that may be lurking just below the surface to give an extra charge to the word. Besides meaning "of two or more colors in blotches," "pied" can be the past tense and the past participle of the verb "to pi" meaning "to spill or throw type into disorder." This sense of disorder might seem to go against the idea of beauty the poem otherwise presents, but if we think of a poem like "Inversnaid" I believe we have to recognize that the wild disorder of nature, as if it were pied or spilled into a naturally disordered order, did strongly appeal to Hopkins:

> What would the world be, once bereft
> Of wet and wildness? Let them be left,
> O let them be left, wildness and wet;
> Long live the weeds and the wilderness yet.

Like "pied," "dappled" is an uncommon common word: we all know what it means but we seldom have occasion to use the word—that is to say, we seldom have occasion to use it unless we happen to be Gerard Manley Hopkins, and then we make of it an "arch-especial" word. "Dapple" or "dappled" occurs occasionally in Hopkins's "Journal"—"Pendle dappled with tufted shadow," "trees when they dapple their boles in wearing its own shadow," "the wind . . . dappled very sweetly on one's face," "The sun itself and the spot of 'session' dappled with big laps and flowers-in-damask of cloud" (*Journals and Papers*, pp. 206, 231, 233, 236)—but it is in the poems that the word comes really into its own and becomes so distinctively Hopkinsian, often—and this is again distinctive—as part of a compound. In a very early fragment, written when Hopkins was twenty years old and after only his first year at Oxford, we hear of "Distance / Dappled with di-minish'd trees / Spann'd with shadow every one" (*Journals and Papers*, p. 31); in "The Wreck of the Deutschland" Hopkins kisses his "hand to the dappled-with-damson west"; in the first lines of "The Windhover" he catches "this morning morning's min-ion, king- / dom of daylight's dauphin, dapple-dawn-drawn Fal-con"; in "Duns Scotus's Oxford," that city has "the dapple-eared lily below" it; "Morning, Midday, and Evening Sacrifice" begins with "The dappled die-away / Cheek and the wimpled lip"; in "Inversnaid," "Degged with dew, dappled with dew / Are the groins of the braes that the brook treads through"; and in the late "Spelt from Sibyl's Leaves" Hopkins mourns the loss of all the dappled things he had praised nine years earlier in "Pied Beauty":

> For earth her being has unbound; her dapple is at end, as-
> Tray or aswarm, all throughther, in throngs; self in self steeped and pashed—quite
> Disremembering, dismembering all now.

One could almost read an aesthetic, moral, and spiritual auto-biography in the variations that Hopkins plays on this single word "dapple," a word that in the end is so much his own that one hardly recognizes it in another poet. "Dapple" is also one of those words that has within itself a subtle tendency to strangeness; at first familiar, if said over a number of times to oneself, it becomes distinctly unfamiliar and strange and in its strange, unfamiliar familiarity one feels almost returned to the beginnings of language.

On the second line of the poem we might content ourselves with quoting the editor of Hopkins's poetry, Norman H. Mac-Kenzie: "Who else [but Hopkins] would be eccentric enough to praise God for skies like a *brinded cow*?"[4] Who, indeed?, but "brinded," which is an ancient or archaic version of "brindled" and thus returns to the language a word all but lost, joins with such other "counter, original, spare, strange" words as "couple-colour," "stipple," "fickle," "freckle," "adazzle," "dim" to compose a dappled hymn of praise that imitates the beauty it celebrates. Similarly, "couple-colour," "rose-moles," "fresh-firecoal," "chestnut-falls," and "fathers-forth," which are all unique Hopkinsian compounds but formed according to regular principles of the language, condense into single words images and meanings of diversity and richness. That Hopkins had a fondness for "all trades, their gear and tackle and trim" is apparent in journal entries where he says over to himself the words with specialized meaning he has heard ("fold" in the previous line, for example: "Br. Sidgreaves has heard the high ridges of a field called *folds* and the hollow between the *drip*" [*Journals and Papers*, p. 191]); and in the line itself he states a principle that Whitman carried very effectively into practice, using the semitechnical language of "all trades, their gear and tackle and trim" to create a special kind of oddness, a little jolt of surprise for the reader in coming upon such "unpoetic" language in poetry. And finally Hopkins gives his language an extra twist in the final words, "Praise him," which, coming after the colon, must be understood to be both indicative and imperative: all these dappled things do praise him; and, Reader, since he fathers-forth all this pied beauty, you must praise him. Given that "Pied Beauty" is one of the least complex and least strange of Hopkins's poems, one must imagine the degree of strangeness, or in his own word "oddness," that he brings to the language of "The Wreck of the Deutschland" or "Spelt from Sibyl's Leaves."

Here is another little poem with "dappled" in it:

> Their dappled importunity
> Disparage or dismiss—
> The Obloquies of Etiquette
> Are obsolete to Bliss—

I remarked a moment ago that "dapple" or "dappled" is so much a Hopkins word that coming upon it in another poet we hardly recognize it, and I think it requires an almost heroic readjustment of eyes and mind—if, indeed, it is possible at all—to recognize Hopkins's "dappled" in this "dappled" of Emily Dickinson. I am not aware that any commentator has had anything to say about this very brief poem (#1611), but I cannot think that the absence of commentary is due to its not being thoroughly Dickinsonian and as strange as it is Dickinsonian. This could not be Hopkins, it could not be Whitman (here is how Whitman's "dappled" sounds: "Flag cerulean—sunny flag, with the orbs of night dappled!" ["Delicate Cluster"]); it is peculiarly Dickinson and could only be her. When she places "dappled" as a modifier for "importunity" Dickinson is using language in a way that neither Hopkins nor Whitman—and no other poet that I can think of—would use it. This is to say that strangeness, to remain strangeness, must be specific and intrinsic to the individual: it cannot be shared around and be imitated or it ceases to be strangeness. Now fashion dictates that the fashionable seek to be a little strange, presumably in order to stand out, to be striking; but fashion quickly shades over into fad, and soon the fashionable are all strange in the same way—which is to say not strange at all. It is otherwise, however, with poets like Dickinson, Hopkins, and Whitman: each of them is strange, very strange, mysteriously strange, and altogether in her/his own way. Dickinson's way for making strange—or I should say one of her ways, for she has many—is to use words, some common, some uncommon, but words that one can find in the dictionary in either case, in the most unusual and improbable of contexts, so that the reader must rethink the meaning of the words entirely. When we come across "dapple-dawn-drawn Falcon" in Hopkins we have to pause a moment to sort out the connections made by the hyphens in order to see that the phrase may mean that the falcon is drawn or etched sharply against the dappled dawn or, alternatively, that the falcon has been drawn out of or attracted from its eyrie by the beauty of the dappled dawn; we must pause for the sense of the phrase, but not for long, and it is the same with other dapples in Hopkins—the dapple-eared lily and the braes dappled with dew and earth's dapple that ends with night and all dappled things of nature: We can understand all of these easily enough. But a "dappled importunity"? What does she *mean*? And "Obloquies of Etiquette" that "Are obsolete to Bliss—"? Hopkins's lily, braes, dew, and earth are physical objects in nature to which he attaches the visual, physical attribute of dappling; his substantives and attributes, being of the same physical realm, go together naturally to form a metonymic description of natural phenomena. But Dickinson's "importunity," "Obloquies," "Etiquette," "obsolete," and "Bliss" are all abstractions of quite another realm from dappling or any other physical attributes. Coming upon "dappled importunity" the reader is forced not only to pause but to stop dead still—and even then I am not sure that the phrase will yield recoverable meaning. Which is to say that I do not believe that this particular poem is altogether successful in nailing a concrete image to an abstraction, but even if not successful it is otherwise entirely characteristic.

A poem that undoubtedly succeeds at this marriage of the concrete and the abstract is #258 with these first two stanzas:

> There's a certain Slant of light,
> Winter Afternoons —
> That oppresses, like the Heft
> Of Cathedral Tunes —
>
> Heavenly Hurt, it gives us —
> We can find no scar,
> But internal difference,
> Where the Meanings are —

The first verb, "oppresses," in its literal and extended meaning, carries the very sense of the poem. To oppress, etymologically and literally, is to press against physically, and that "a certain Slant of light, / Winter afternoons" can do this, can press against us and affect us physically, is a strange but exact paradox. In an extended sense, but not so far extended as to lose this literal sense, to oppress means to weigh on or to burden (one cannot avoid the physical metaphor) mentally or spiritually, and this is what the poem is about. The word that one thinks of as particularly Dickinsonian, however, and that performs this same metaphoric task of joining the physical and the spiritual, is "Heft." It may be that the word seems Dickinsonian only because her first editors changed it to "weight," but returning to the original "heft" feels like having Dickinson back again in the poem, and "the Heft / Of Cathedral Tunes" has just the right mix of experience common and available to all of us — Cathedral Tunes are supposed to lift us or heave us up but in fact too often weigh us down — and hints of the strange and mysterious. "Heft" gives a little shock of delight as an attribute of "Cathedral Tunes." "Weight" does not have the mixed colloquial and strange — strange *because* colloquial and seen anew — quality about it that "heft" has.

Dickinson gets much the same effect with the same word in poem #632:

> The Brain—is wider than the Sky—
> For—put them side by side—
> The one the other will contain
> With ease—and You—beside—
>
> The Brain is deeper than the sea—
> For—hold them—Blue to Blue—
> The one the other will absorb—
> As Sponges—Buckets—do—
>
> The Brain is just the weight of God—
> For—Heft them—Pound for Pound—
> And they will differ—if they do—
> As Syllable from Sound—

It is a wonderfully physical act this hefting of the brain and God. Who but Dickinson would think of the bizarre notion of taking the brain in one hand and God in the other and trying them comparatively, pound for pound, to see which has the greater heft? And the equation established by this act of hefting—the brain is to God as syllable is to sound—is equally Dickinsonian and equally fascinating and bold. Syllable is an instance of sound, it is sound realized, and without syllable sound is but a word or a concept. The difference, or the relationship, is the same as that drawn by linguists between *parole* and *langue*, where the latter, *langue*, is a language system and *parole* is a language event or utterance. But is not this very poem we are looking at a language event or utterance? Is it not what we might call an act of syllabled sound? And is not Dickinson, then, saying this?—"Take this poem and the weight of God and heft them pound for pound and see which, if either of them, kicks the beam: It will not be the poem." This high valuation placed on poetry as a creation of the human brain is not uncommon in Dickinson. Poem #945, for example, begins

by characterizing a poem or other work of art as "a Blossom of
the Brain" and concludes with meditation on what its loss would
mean: "When it is lost, that Day shall be / The Funeral of God."

The great and peculiar word—peculiar as she uses it, not peculiar in itself—for the grandeur of her art, as all readers of Dickinson know, is "circumference," which meant to her something like
the infinite reach of the poet's consciousness and the promise
of immortality for her verse. Higginson might smile at her, she
wrote to him in a letter, but "I could not stop for that—My Business is Circumference—" (*Letters*, #268), and a grand Business it
was too.

> She staked her Feathers—Gained an Arc—
> Debated—Rose again—
> This time—beyond the estimate
> Of Envy, or of Men—
>
> And now, among Circumference—
> Her steady Boat be seen—
> At home—among the Billows—As
> The Bough where she was born—

The Arc that she gains in her first try at her Business is like a
little section of the entire Circumference, and that in itself is a
considerable achievement, but not to be compared with her second attempt, rising "beyond the estimate / Of Envy, or of Men."
And now she has it all, being both a seabird and a songbird,
at home "among the Billows" and on the bough, but most at
home in her native habitat "among Circumference." For someone
who even some years later would wear the mask of a little girl
humbly seeking the help of—as she called him—her Preceptor
(i.e., T. W. Higginson), Dickinson is remarkably, even astonishingly self-assured and self-confident in a poem like this one. But
this same note of assurance and certainty of vocation is really just
below the surface in the letters to Higginson also where Dickin-

son, when she is not posing as "Your Scholar" or "Your Gnome," signs herself, with authorial grandeur, simply "Dickinson," and seems to say, "You can smile if you want, but my Business is Circumference and I know what I am about."⁵ And she did, too, as in poem #633:

> When Bells stop ringing—Church—begins—
> The Positive—of Bells—
> When Cogs—stop—that's Circumference—
> The Ultimate—of Wheels.

The poem is virtually unparaphrasable, and this is one mark of Dickinson's greatness, that what she had to say could be said in no other way at all than the way it is said in the poems. And who else would think to say, or feel compelled to say, that Church is the Positive of Bells or Circumference the Ultimate of Wheels? Church is the positive, the apotheosis or the telos, of bells, the end toward which bells move or to which they aspire; so also with Circumference, the ultimate, the perfected state that endlessly turning wheels strive to achieve. But neither bells nor wheels will ever attain the stilled, perfected condition of church or circumference, not until cogs, that swing the bells, turn the wheels, and move the hands of time, stop; and that instant will usher in church, circumference, and eternity. In the Platonic dialogue that bears his name, Timaeus says that "time is a moving image of eternity," and from Dickinson's poem we might say that bells, in just the same way, are a moving image of church and wheels a moving image of circumference. Saying so much, and honoring Dickinson's assertion that her business is circumference, we must recognize that Dickinson makes very great claims—claims even of immortality and eternity—for poetry as a kind of human achievement of divine proportions forever there in the sum of the universe.

But it is the poem, not the poet, that lasts, as Dickinson insists in #883:

The Poets light but Lamps—
Themselves—go out—
The Wicks they stimulate—
If vital Light

Inhere as do the Suns—
Each Age a Lens
Disseminating their
Circumference—

Translated, I suppose one could say that this poem "means" that art is long, life is short, that poems that are successful are as everlasting as the sun, and that each succeeding age is illuminated, according to its specific needs and its best understanding, by the poem, which is itself unchanging. But Dickinson must be one of the most difficult poets in the language to translate, and this "translation" does no more than state an idea that may be lurking around the poem somewhere but is not at all, or in any way, the poem itself. Dickinson uses language—words—in such odd, tangential ways, always just slightly off to the side of their dictionary definitions, that a translator would be driven to ultimate frustration by trying for some sort of exact correspondence between what the words are known to mean from a dictionary and what those same words signify in Dickinson's own private lexicon. She remarked in a letter to Higginson that after her first "Tutor" died, "for several years, my Lexicon—was my only companion" (*Letters*, p. 172), but I think it fair to say that she infused as much private meaning into the words of the Lexicon as she drew public meaning out of it. Looking only to a dictionary definition of the verb, I cannot see that one would ever "stimulate" a wick, nor do I think that, lexically speaking, light would "inhere as do the Suns." And as for each age being "a Lens / Disseminating their / Circumference," it is brilliant and impossible and very Emily Dickinson. Each age as a lens is fine, no problem, but there is a seed planted right in the middle of "disseminating" (from *dis-* + *seminare* to sow, from *semin, semen* seed), and how a lens is going to sow the seed of the circumference of the wicks is beyond me, and beyond the dictionary too, but I admire the poem nonetheless, and my admiration is not diminished but increased by its strangeness and oddity.

Whitman made strange with words in other ways than either Hopkins or Dickinson, but he did make strange alright. I remarked earlier that the word "heft" was a word that Dickinson made peculiarly her own, but that prevented neither Hopkins nor Whitman from doing their own will on the word. Hopkins uses the word in the poem titled "On the Portrait of Two Beautiful Young People" to describe the brother and sister of the title and their parents:

> Happy the father, mother of these! Too fast:
> Not that, but thus far, all with frailty, blest
> In one fair fall; but, for time's aftercast,
> Creatures all heft, hope, hazard, interest.

This quatrain, as one might well imagine it would do, sends Hopkins's editor in the Oxford Authors Series scrambling for a footnote—and it seems to me a very good footnote, translating Hopkins back to acceptable dictionary sense: "Perhaps," Catherine Phillips cautiously says, "Perhaps, [it means] as for the future, the children will be (for their parents) a source of effort, hope, risk, and interest,"[6] and this, I think, is a useful gloss on a passage that otherwise risks being in a language that is altogether too private. Whitman's way with "heft" is more interesting than Hopkins's in my opinion—indeed I find it virtually as interesting as Dickinson's way with the word. I must quote at some length from "Song of Myself" because "heft" (or "hefts" rather) occurs in the middle of a passage that begins with Whitman doting on himself and ends with nothing less than an orgasmic sunrise.

> I dote on myself, there is that lot of me and all so luscious,
> Each moment and whatever happens thrills me with joy,

I cannot tell how my ankles bend, nor whence the cause of my
   faintest wish,
Nor the cause of the friendship I emit, nor the cause of the
   friendship I take again.

That I walk up my stoop, I pause to consider if it really be,
A morning-glory at my window satisfies me more than the
   metaphysics of books.

To behold the day-break!
The little light fades the immense and diaphanous shadows,
The air tastes good to my palate.

Hefts of the moving world at innocent gambols silently rising,
   freshly exuding,
Scooting obliquely high and low.

Something I cannot see puts upward libidinous prongs,
Seas of bright juice suffuse heaven.

I am not sure of the innocence of those gambols that the "hefts
of the moving world" are up to, gambols that result in upward
thrusting "libidinous prongs" and "seas of bright juice" suffusing
heaven, but it is all of a piece with Whitman doting on himself
and on the fact that "there is that lot of me and all so luscious."
Whitman in this passage is very much at one with "hefts of the
moving world" at gambols, innocent or otherwise.

   "Heft" or "hefts" is the kind of word that one expects in
Whitman, a sturdy old word that with its cognates, "heave" and
"heavy," goes back to Old English and Old High German and
perhaps to a Latin source even earlier. But if "hefts" is the kind of
word one expects in Whitman, then what are we to say of a very
different kind of vocabulary in this passage—the vocabulary of
"luscious" and "diaphanous" and "gambols" and "libidinous" and
"suffuse"? None of these words have a particularly Anglo-Saxon
feel about them; they all seem as if they might be out of a different dictionary than the one that has "hefts" in it. The truth is

that Whitman's vocabulary is much richer and much more varied than one often thinks—more varied than Dickinson or Hopkins I believe—and Whitman draws from all sorts of sources and from many levels of usage, deliberately juxtaposing contrary sources and usage levels to create a wondrous strange effect in the poetry. One source of vocabulary in Whitman is his love of "all trades, their gear and tackle and trim"; the catalogues of his "Song for Occupations," for example, revel in the language of trades, for as the poem says, "Strange and hard that paradox true I give, / Objects gross and the unseen soul are one." Hence the listing of objects gross to realize the strange paradox that they are one with the unseen soul:

> The blast-furnace and the puddling-furnace, the loup-lump at
>   the bottom of the melt at last, the rolling-mill, the stumpy
>   bars of pig-iron, the strong, clean-shaped T-rail for
>   railroads . . . ,
> The calking-iron, the kettle of boiling vault-cement, and the
>   fire under the kettle,
> The cotton-bale, the stevedore's hook, the saw and buck of
>   the sawyer, the mould of the moulder, the working-knife
>   of the butcher, the ice-saw, and all the work with ice,
> The work and tools of the rigger, grappler, sail-maker,
>   block-maker . . . ,
> The awl and knee-strap, the pint measure and quart measure,
>   the counter and stool, the writing-pen of quill or metal, the
>   making of all sorts of edged tools . . .

and so on and on and on to the significance of it all:

> The hourly routine of your own or any man's life, the shop,
>   yard, store, or factory,
> These shows all near you by day and night—workman!
>   whoever you are, your daily life!
> In that and them the heft of the heaviest—in that and them far
>   more than you estimated, (and far less also,)

In them realities for you and me, in them poems for you and
  me. . . .[7]

Central of course to Whitman's notion of the business of the
Great American Poet was the idea that the truest poetry was to
be found in objects and activities and persons and language heretofore considered entirely unpoetic; and certainly in passages like
the foregoing he justifies his claim to be doing something different
and original by bringing the low, the "gross," the common and
ordinary into poetry. This is the same tactic Whitman spells out
in "Song of Myself" where he insists that no one will be turned
away from his feast — in particular, in addition to the kept woman,
the sponger, and the thief, he says, "the venerealee is invited" (section 19). Only Whitman. . . . The strange word is even hard to say
and must have been original with Whitman, though once he had
created the word "venerealee" and introduced it into the polite
poetic society of "Song of Myself," he seems to have been quite
pleased with himself, for he uses it again in "The Sleepers" ("The
child of the glutton or the venerealee waits long . . .") and once
more in "A Hand-Mirror" ("A drunkard's breath, unwholesome
eater's face, venerealee's flesh . . .").[8] When the "unpoetic" thus
pushes its head up through the pages of *Leaves of Grass*, the reader
is intended, I believe, to experience — and does experience — a little
frisson of surprise and dismay and delight.

I use the word *frisson* rather than an English equivalent —
"shiver" or "thrill" or "shudder" — deliberately and with Whitman's implied warrant, for this most American of poets was not
content to restrict himself to the vocabulary of the language that
he declared "befriends the grand American expression."[9] Henry
James might deplore "his too-extensive acquaintance with the foreign languages," but Whitman went his merry and peculiar way
all the same, throwing in the odd foreign word at strange and
unexpected moments. "Passage O soul to India!" he exclaims:
"Eclaircise the myths Asiatic, the primitive fables." It is not "light
up" or "illumine" but "eclaircise the myths Asiatic," and of course,

even if it seems crazy at first, Whitman is right: Every reader of "Passage to India" must remember this bizarre line at the beginning of the second section of the poem, while a tamer line — without the "eclaircise" and the inversion in "myths Asiatic" — would scarcely be remembered by anyone. The entire body of his work, the corollary and complement of his life, Whitman says in a very late poem with a characteristically Whitmanian title and first line — "On, On the Same, Ye Jocund Twain!" — has been a "strange *eclaircissement* of all the masses past, the eastern world, the ancient, medieval," etc. In a similar foreign vein, comrades are often "camerados" in Whitman ("As I Lay with My Head in Your Lap Camerado"); the Lord is "the great Camerado," upper-case C ("Song of Myself," section 45); and friends or lovers are not just "friends" or "lovers" but "amies":

> Partaker of influx and efflux I, extoller of hate and conciliation,
> Extoller of amies and those that sleep in each others' arms. . . .
> ("Song of Myself," section 22)

Whitman himself was not only a "camerado" and an "ami" but also "a real Parisian": "I am a habitan of Vienna, St. Petersburg, Berlin, Constantinople," and some twenty-five other outlandish cities, he declares in the poem called "Salut au Monde!" (section 9); he was a "chansonnier" as well ("The Centenarian's Story") who "blabb'd" ("Crossing Brooklyn Ferry") and "promulged" himself ("Song of Myself," section 45), in season and out, on the "trottoirs" of Manahatta ("Manahatta") and everywhere else he had been a "habitan" of — all this, of course, when he was not being, or in addition to being, a "kosmos." Well might Whitman himself term it "a strange voice." But stranger yet, all these foreign and exotic words are cheek by jowl with those great short lines of simplest utterance in Whitman:

> All this I swallow, it tastes good, I like it well, it becomes mine,
> I am the man, I suffer'd, I was there.

> All these I feel or am.

The hiss of the surgeon's knife, the gnawing teeth of his saw,
Wheeze, cluck, swash of falling blood, short wild scream, and
   long, dull, tapering groan,
These so, these irretrievable.

> ("Song of Myself," sections 33, 36)

Whitman himself has the best comment on this language from "Song of Myself," and it comes in "Song of Myself" (section 8): "What living and buried speech," he says, "is always vibrating here."

One other feature of Whitman's vocabulary that makes him sound like himself and no one else is his choice, and sometimes creation, of words, in "Song of Myself" in particular but elsewhere as well, that in their formation and sound, in their oral shaping, enact what they signify. I have in mind especially a kind of structure of sound that he builds up around words centering on "o" sounds and that seem to "mean" something like the rounded, enfolding, expansive quality of "o"-ness. Thus we have, all from "Song of Myself," words like "omnific" and "omnigenous" (these first two are, I believe, Whitman coinages, and I do not even know how to pronounce the second of them) and "Omnivorous":

And they are to branch boundlessly out of that lesson until it
   becomes omnific,
And until one and all shall delight us, and we them.

> (section 30)

Myself moving forward then and now and forever,
Gathering and showing more always and with velocity,
Infinite and omnigenous, and the like of these among them. . . .

> (section 32)

I know perfectly well my own egotism,
Know my omnivorous lines and must not write any less,
And would fetch you whoever you are flush with myself.

> (section 42)

Like these "omni-" words that would take all into their embrace, there are words that refer directly to the rounding of sound in the mouth—"orotund" (from *ore rotundo*, with round mouth) and "embouchure" (from *en bouche*, in the mouth):

> A call in the midst of the crowd,
> My own voice, orotund sweeping and final.
>
> (section 42)
>
> I beat and pound for the dead,
> I blow through my embouchures my loudest
>   and gayest for them.
>
> (section 18)

In addition, we have words like "orbit" ("I know that this orbit of mine cannot be swept by a carpenter's compass"—section 20), "orbic" ("A tenor loud and fresh as the creation fills me, / The orbic flex of his mouth is pouring and filling me full"—section 26), and "orb" or "orbs" ("For it the nebula cohered to an orb"—section 44; "the enfolders of those orbs"—section 46; "I, turning, call to thee O soul, thou actual Me, / And lo, thou gently master-est the orbs"—"Passage to India," section 8). What these orotund orbs are forever about is rounding themselves out to larger and larger O's until they become vast rondures enfolding and enclosing all. "Our own rondure, the current globe I bring," Whitman says in "Song of the Exposition"; and in "Passage to India" he proclaims the "rondure of the world at last accomplish'd. / O vast Rondure, swimming in space, / Cover'd all over with visible power and beauty. . . ." One of the great words in Whitman is just this little, single-letter word "o"—"O death," "O my soul," "O vast Rondure." Surely this vast Rondure, introduced by and imitating its "O," is nothing less than a kosmos—*the* Kosmos—and "It is no small matter," Whitman says in another poem ("Who Learns My Lesson Complete"), "this round and delicious globe moving so exactly in its orbit for ever and ever." Everywhere Whitman's verse, in word, in line, and in statement, rounds itself omnifically, omnigenously, omnivorously, orbically outward:

Wider and wider they spread, expanding, always expanding,
Outward and outward and forever outward.
                        ("Song of Myself," section 45)

What happens here is that vocabulary, like everything else in
Whitman, gradually and insensibly expands to take on syntactic, formal, and thematic significance. The line imitates the word,
the poem imitates the line, and *Leaves of Grass* itself is an imitation of word, line, and poem. This expansion outward, outward,
outward until

Rounded by thee in one — one common orbic language,
One common indivisible destiny for All,
                    ("Song of the Exposition," section 8)

is the characteristic and distinctive mark of Whitman's poetry
everywhere. It is how he attains to Dickinsonian Circumference.

But this is one of the paradoxes of making strange, for Emily
Dickinson stamps her poetry with distinctiveness and achieves
Circumference just as surely and effectively as Whitman but in
exactly the opposite way, not through dilation, swelling, and expanding but through condensation, compaction, and elliptical
compression. Cooks speak of "reducing" sauces, meaning not only
that they boil off the liquid to diminish the quantity of sauce but
also that they thereby concentrate the flavor and texture of the
sauce. In this sense, Dickinson's is a poetry of reduction — even,
I would say, of extreme and drastic reduction. Not only are her
lines mostly short and her forms very tight, but in the process
of composition she frequently boils away all of those grammatical and logical connectives that to her mind are as unnecessary
and as unwanted as excess liquid in a cook's sauce but whose absence puts the reader to the severe test of trying to puzzle out
how a Dickinson poem gets from its opening line — usually very
startling in itself — to its concluding line; and not only that, for
this kind of difficulty is to be found in most poems of depth and
complexity by poets other than Dickinson, but it is often difficult

to negotiate in her poems the passage from any one line to the
next because Dickinson has removed the connectives, if there ever
were any, that would show the logical and grammatical relation-
ships between the two lines. Hopkins has been called a difficult
poet, and in certain ways he is, but the difficulty his poetry offers
is of quite another order from the difficulty of Dickinson's poems.
(For what it's worth, and by way of contrast, I do not believe
that most people find Whitman a difficult poet.) The difficulty
that Hopkins presents is, in a sense, merely incidental, due to
his overloading a relatively simple subject or idea with a burden
of elaborations and complexities that it cannot sustain; the difficulty in Dickinson, on the other hand, is essential and of the very
nature of her poetry. To put the contrast in a rather simple way I
would say that, no matter how complicated their surface might be,
Hopkins could always say what his poems meant, Dickinson never
could (except in such formulations as "My Business is Circumference"). Poems like "Harry Ploughman" and "Tom's Garland,"
which Robert Bridges and Richard Watson Dixon found it difficult
and even impossible to understand, Hopkins could "explain" and
could say very clearly what they "meant." Sending the two poems
to Dixon, Hopkins called them "works of infinite, of over great
contrivance, I am afraid, to the annulling in the end of the right
effect" (*Correspondence of GMH and RWD*, p. 153). When he heard
from Bridges that he could not understand "Harry Ploughman,"
Hopkins responded, "The difficulties are of syntax no doubt," and
he admitted that "[d]ividing a compound word by a clause sand-
wiched into it was a desperate deed . . . and I do not feel that it
was an unquestionable success" (*Letters to RB*, p. 265). And when
he discovered that Bridges and Dixon were writing one another
in a futile effort to find out what "Tom's Garland" was about his
reaction was both characteristic and revealing: "I laughed out-
right," Hopkins wrote to Bridges, "and often, but very sardon-
ically, to think you and the Canon could not construe my last
sonnet; that he had to write to you for a crib. It is plain I must

go no farther on this road: if you and he cannot understand me who will? . . . Must I interpret it? It means then that . . ." (*Letters to RB*, p. 272). There follows then an explanation of nearly two printed pages saying exactly and in detail what the twenty-line poem means. In the middle of the explanation, Hopkins exclaims, perhaps with some irony, "O, once explained, how clear it all is!"; and indeed he does make clear what the paraphrasable meaning or the intention of the poem is. Not that we can take this to be the equivalent of the poem itself, for what Hopkins does in effect is to shear away all the elaborations of sound and the twisted syntactical constructions that are so distinctively Hopkinsian to get to the bare-bones idea from which the poem started or on which the poem has been structured. But even when we acknowledge this, we have still to recognize that Hopkins can do something and does do something that Dickinson never does and never could do: say what a poem "means." In fact, in discussing the meaning of "Harry Ploughman" with Bridges, Hopkins proposed doing just that for a number of his poems, saying what any given poem means in an "argument" outside the poem itself. After troubling over how he might introduce syntactical notations that would indicate which words are to be taken for subject, verb, object, and so on—not always a clear matter in Hopkins (or Dickinson)— he suddenly thinks of a general solution to the kind of difficulty "Harry Ploughman" and "Tom's Garland" pose:

But however that reminds me that one thing I am now resolved on, it is to prefix short prose *arguments* to some of my pieces. These too will expose me to carping, but I do not mind. Epic and drama and ballad and many, most, things should be at once intelligible; but everything need not and cannot be. Plainly if it is possible to express a subtle and recondite thought on a subtle and recondite subject in a subtle and recondite way and with great felicity and perfection, in the end, something must be sacrificed, with so trying a task, in the process, and this may be the being at once, nay perhaps even the being without explanation at all, intelligible. Neither, in the same light, does it seem to be to me a real objection . . . that the argument should be even longer than the piece; for the merit of the work may lie for one thing in its terseness (*Letters to RB*, pp. 265–66).

There is a good deal of special pleading going on in this letter, especially in light of the poem that sparked it off, for "Harry Ploughman" is not on a subtle and recondite subject but is simply a Whitmanlike description of a ploughman; the important point, however, is that Hopkins should propose prefixing an argument to some of his poems, that he could perfectly well have done so, and that such an external explanation would ease the task of the reader mightily (though it might also reveal, in instances like "Harry Ploughman," that there is not as much substance to the poem as "contrivance").

Most readers would welcome an argument prefixed to a poem like "Tom's Garland," and they can imagine what such an argument might look like since Hopkins wrote one in a long letter to Bridges (*Letters to RB*, pp. 272–74). But no one, I should think, could imagine what kind of argument might be prefixed to Dickinson's poem #1072:

> Title divine — is mine!
> The Wife — without the Sign!
> Acute Degree — conferred on me —
> Empress of Calvary!
> Royal — all but the Crown!
> Betrothed — without the swoon
> God sends us Women —
> When you — hold — Garnet to Garnet —
> Gold — to Gold —
> Born — Bridalled — Shrouded —
> In a Day —

Tri Victory
"My Husband"—women say—
Stroking the Melody—
Is *this*—the way?

For oddity and difficulty, Hopkins cannot hold a candle to Dickinson. What kind of "argument" could she prefix to this poem? The poem was written at just about the time Dickinson commenced correspondence with Higginson and one is pleased to wonder what her response would have been had she sent the poem to Higginson and had he asked for an explanation. Would she, like Hopkins, have said, "Must I interpret it? It means then that . . . ," etc.? We need not wonder long, however, for as it happens Dickinson sent this poem in a letter—actually it is almost the entire letter—to Samuel Bowles, adding, after the poem, only this very brief note, as cryptic as the poem itself: "Here's—what I had to 'tell you'—You will tell no other? Honor—is it's [*sic*] own pawn—" (*Letters*, #250). Surely Dickinson was safe in confiding in Bowles, for what, given this poem, would he have told anyone? that Dickinson possessed the "Title divine"? that she was "The Wife—without the Sign"? that she was "Empress of Calvary . . . Born—Bridalled—Shrouded— / In a Day—"? Not likely, but there were no other terms for it: what she had to "tell" Bowles, what she has to tell us, her readers, could only be told in this way. When I say that there are no other terms for it, or that the poem cannot be paraphrased, I do not mean, of course, that there are not interesting things to observe and to say about the poem. It is, for example, pertinent to observe that Dickinson frequently imagines love as the equivalent of Christ's suffering on Calvary, and that this poem, in which she figures herself as "Empress of Calvary," was written in 1862, that *annus mirabilis* that records something awesome and terrible that happened to Dickinson and within her—no one knows what exactly—and that impelled her to an overwhelming rush of poetry as her only hold on reality in a time of fearful crisis. (Thomas H. Johnson says that "[d]uring that year she copied into the packets no fewer than three hundred and sixty-six poems, the greater part of them complete and final texts" [*Emily Dickinson: An Interpretive Biography*, p. 73].) Much could be said, too, about the punctuation of these lines—not just the dashes, though these also, but the exclamation marks that give the first lines their extraordinary shrill intensity. And then there is the fantastic central phrase, central to this poem and central to Dickinson's vision of marriage: "Born—Bridalled—Shrouded— / In a Day—" To call this a "Tri Victory"—well, what can one say but "strange victory" and "only in Dickinson": many more victories like this one and she could about pack it in. If one takes this poem together with the other highly peculiar "marriage poems" (as they have been called), there would be much to say about Dickinson's psychological and emotional makeup and its translation into language as bizarre as the complex emotional state itself. And finally there are the eerie and wonderful last lines with their apparent contempt for women who are in a conventionally married state rather than, like Dickinson, in a unique husband-less married state: " 'My Husband'—women say— / Stroking the Melody— / Is *this*—the way?" But saying all these things does not in any way replace the poem or say what it "means"; only the poem says what it means; it is what Dickinson had to tell Bowles and what she has to tell us.

In poems like "Harry Ploughman" and "Tom's Garland," and more successfully in poems like "The Wreck of the Deutsch-land" and "Spelt from Sibyl's Leaves," Hopkins makes strange and makes difficulty for the reader by laying it on; in a poem like "Title divine—is mine!" Dickinson makes strange and makes difficulty by taking away. Yet both poets, in contrast to Whitman, achieve effects of great intensity in their poetry through the compression that comes with formal constraints. Subjecting the emotional matter of a poem to the formal demands of rhyme, meter, and stanza design both contains the emotion and at the same time increases its force. I take it that this is one of the ideas behind a poem like Dickinson's #1247, one of her "poems of definition," this time a definition of poetry itself and simultaneously of its "coeval" partner, love:

> To pile like Thunder to its close
> Then crumble grand away
> While Everything created hid
> This—would be Poetry—
>
> Or Love—the two coeval come—
> We both and neither prove—
> Experience either and consume—
> For None see God and live—

Poetry here is not so much the particular instance of poetry, the individual poem, as it is the Platonic Idea or Form of poetry, sheer poetry one might say, poetry as the perfect "Adequate" of consciousness and emotional experience. As such, and for Dickinson, it is precisely the coeval of Love—something that we cannot prove, that we cannot know, that we cannot experience and live on in the ordinary way of living on. Yet poem #1247, while informed by this notion of poetry, is itself a poem, i.e., a formed, shaped, controlled artifact, and this is the paradox of this poem as an instance of poetry. Poetry in itself, in its essence, as the first line says, is "To pile like Thunder to its close"; it is like a thunderstroke, explosive, shattering, formless, crumbling "grand away." But the fourth and fifth lines present this idea in a peculiarly Dickinsonian way—hesitantly, with the dashes restraining any rush of affirmation, and subjunctively, with the verbs asserting something only of a world or context that is not the present one: "This— *would be* poetry"—not *is* poetry, but *would be*; and in a world where this poetry is rather than would be, love would coeval come. The point might be made in another way with reference to Dickinson's punctuation, in particular her use of capital letters (but I am not suggesting that this is intended by Dickinson, for her use of capitals for nouns is too frequent for this to be an intended significance in any isolated case). The following line—"We both and neither prove"—we might gloss by saying that we are capable of proving both poetry and love as lower-case experiences, as poems and as loves, but of proving neither of them as upper-case Poetry and Love. This produces the perfect ambiguity of the next line— "Experience either and consume." The dictionary offers two possible definitions for "consume" that would be pertinent here: the first is as a transitive verb and means "to engage fully," in which case the verbs would be imperative and would instruct or enjoin us to experience and engage fully both poetry and love; the second is as an intransitive verb and means "to perish," in which case the verbs would be indicative and would simply say that to experience either Poetry or Love would be to perish. "To pile like Thunder to its close," as poem and poetry, manages to have it both ways at once.

This strategy of containing explosive emotional content within quite strict formal bounds, thereby paradoxically increasing its potency while simultaneously diminishing its danger, is common to both Dickinson and Hopkins and the contrary of Whitman's way. Whitman exercises only very light formal restraints, giving the explosive content its head and letting it all—or almost all— hang out in his long, expansive lines and expansive poems. Hopkins may seem to do this too in such poems as "The Leaden Echo and the Golden Echo" or "To What Serves Mortal Beauty" with their Whitmanesque long lines and parallel repetitions, or again in a poem like "Harry Ploughman" with its Whitmanlike description of someone at his occupation (of the latter poem Hopkins wrote to Bridges that it "is a direct picture of a ploughman, without afterthought. But when you read it let me know if there is anything like it in Walt Whitman, as perhaps there may be, and I should be sorry for that" [*Letters to RB*, p. 262]). I believe that this would be a mistaken perception, however, and that with regard to constraining formal patterns Hopkins is much closer to Dickinson than to Whitman — or indeed on the other side of Dickinson from Whitman. Hopkins was unquestionably right when he referred to his verse as "highly wrought," and I think he was right, too, when he responded to Bridges's charge that there was "no conceivable licence" that could not be justified by Hopkins's poetics with his counterclaim to very great strictness and regularity: "Only remark," Hopkins wrote, "as you say that there is no conceivable licence I shd. not be able to justify, that with all my licences, or rather laws, I am stricter than you and I might say than anybody I know. . . . So that I may say my apparent licences are counterbalanced, and more, by my strictness. In fact all English verse, except Milton's, almost, offends me as 'licentious' " (*Letters to RB*, pp. 44–45). In this respect, with his "highly wrought" verse and his strictness, "or rather laws," Hopkins stands apart from both Dickinson and Whitman: their poems, different as they are in other ways, when put beside Hopkins's, have a distinctly homemade quality about them.

Nevertheless, formal patterning has much the same function in Hopkins as in Dickinson: to increase the emotional intensity by containing it while yet making it expressible. "I had no Monarch in my life," Dickinson wrote to Higginson, "and cannot rule myself, and when I try to organize — my little Force explodes — and leaves me bare and charred—" (*Letters*, #271).[10] Hopkins would no doubt have thought it a delusion to believe that someone else could fill the role of "Monarch" and could "organize" for the poet, but the experience of having the "Force" explode, leaving him "bare and charred," was unquestionably one he was familiar with; but when this happened to him, Hopkins was so practiced in the sonnet, so intimately at one with its formal laws, that the experience resulted in poems of the strictest formal observances controlling matter of the most unruly and explosive, emotional sort. Writing to Bridges of the "sonnets of desolation," Hopkins said, "I have after long silence written two sonnets, which I am

touching: if ever anything was written in blood one of these was"
(*Letters to RB*, p. 219); and several months later, "I shall shortly
have some sonnets to send you, five or more. Four of these came
like inspirations unbidden and against my will" (p. 221). Unbidden and against his will, but sonnets all the same, not chaos and
not just a blind scream. No one is sure exactly which four poems
Hopkins referred to, but I think "No worst" is undoubtedly one
of them:

> No worst, there is none. Pitched past pitch of grief,
> More pangs will, schooled at forepangs, wilder wring.
> Comforter, where, where is your comforting?
> Mary, mother of us, where is your relief?
> My cries heave, herds-long; huddle in a main, a chief-
> Woe, world-sorrow; on an age-old anvil wince and sing—
> Then lull, then leave off. Fury had shrieked 'No ling-
> Ering! Let me be fell: force I must be brief.'
> O the mind, mind has mountains; cliffs of fall
> Frightful, sheer, no-man-fathomed. Hold them cheap
> May who ne'er hung there. Nor does long our small
> Durance deal with that steep or deep. Here! creep,
> Wretch, under a comfort serves in a whirlwind: all
> Life death does end and each day dies with sleep.

To say that this is poetry *in extremis* would hardly be enough; I
think we could well find it *extra extremis*. That "the mind, mind
has mountains; cliffs of fall / Frightful, sheer, no-man-fathomed,"
nor no-woman-fathomed either, would come as no surprise to
Hopkins's companion *in extremis*, Emily Dickinson. She proved
the experience in her life and attempted to define it in her poetry.
As she said in one of her fantastic letters to Higginson—letters so
like her poems that one scarcely knows where one leaves off and
the other takes up—about her state of mind in 1862 and the necessity of poetry: "I had a terror—since September—I could tell to
none—and so I sing, as the Boy does by the Burying Ground—be-

cause I am afraid—" (*Letters*, #261). A striking fact of her singing,
"as the Boy does by the Burying Ground," is the tense, tenuous
control of her material that Dickinson maintains by the regularity
of the form she adopts. A poem like #410, for example, has madness for its subject and the most strictly observed Short Meter
(quatrain stanzas with lines of six, six, eight, and six syllables) for
its form. The rhymes, which, after the first stanza, are only slightly
approximate, suggest the psychic disintegration, barely held off,
that threatens throughout, and the image of the "Brain [that]
keeps giggling—still" has the power to terrify by its own kind of
madness.

> The first Day's Night had come—
> And grateful that a thing
> So terrible—had been endured—
> I told my Soul to sing—
>
> She said her Strings were snapt—
> Her Bow—to Atoms blown—
> And so to mend her—gave me work
> Until another Morn—
>
> And then—a Day as huge
> As Yesterdays in pairs,
> Unrolled its horror in my face—
> Until it blocked my eyes—
>
> My Brain—begun to laugh—
> I mumbled—like a fool—
> And tho' 'tis Years ago—that Day—
> My Brain keeps giggling—still.
>
> And Something's odd—within—
> That person that I was—
> And this One—do not feel the same—
> Could it be Madness—this?

This is an astonishingly assured poem about an experience — that tremendous and terrifying experience to which much of Dickinson's greatest poetry is a response — that one would have thought would have destroyed utterly any assurance Dickinson might have mustered about herself, her life, or her art. It is an assured poem about a condition of total nonassurance, an integrated expression of psychic disintegration — in this way very like Hopkins's "No worst." About the time the late sonnets were coming to Hopkins "unbidden and against my will," he was writing in a postscript to a letter congratulating Bridges on his coming marriage, "I am, I believe, recovering from a deep fit of nervous prostration (I suppose I ought to call it): I did not know but I was dying" (*Letters to RB*, p. 193); though he thought he was recovering at the time of this letter (in 1884), he wrote again to Bridges a year later, in the same letter that mentions the sonnet "written in blood," explaining that the long delay in correspondence from his end "was due to work, worry, and languishment of body and mind — which must be and will be; and indeed to diagnose my own case," Hopkins says, "I think that my fits of sadness, though they do not affect my judgment, resemble madness" (p. 216). It only increases the strangeness and the wonder of it all that these extremes of psychic experience should have found expression in such highly regular, traditional forms as the Italian sonnet (for Hopkins) and the Short Meter hymn (for Dickinson).

There is, of course, a kind of madness, too, about Whitman's poetry, a poetry that pushes to the extreme limits and beyond as much as the poetry of Dickinson and Hopkins. The madness of Whitman's verse has most to do with his insatiate metonymic desire to annex all bodies to his own body as in these separate passages from "Song of Myself":

> Who goes there? hankering, gross, mystical, nude;
> How is it I extract strength from the beef I eat? . . .

Having pried through the strata, analyzed to a hair,
   counsel'd with doctors and calculated close,
I find no sweeter fat than sticks to my own bones.
. . . .
Divine am I inside and out, and I make holy whatever
   I touch or am touch'd from,
The scent of these arm-pits aroma finer than prayer,
This head more than churches, bibles, and all the creeds.
. . . .
Is this then a touch? quivering me to a new identity,
Flames and ether making a rush for my veins,
Treacherous tip of me reaching and crowding to help them,
My flesh and blood playing out lightning to strike what is
   hardly different from myself,
On all sides prurient provokers stiffening my limbs,
Straining the udder of my heart for its withheld drip,
Behaving licentious toward me, taking no denial. . . .
. . . .
I turn the bridegroom out of bed and stay with the bride
   myself,
I tighten her all night to my thighs and lips.
. . . .
On women fit for conception I start bigger and nimbler
   babes,
(This day I am jetting the stuff of far more arrogant
   republics.)
          ("Song of Myself," sections 20, 24, 28, 33, 40)

This hyper-metonymic devouring of the human world and the
universe alike is all crazy, crazy as only Whitman can be and would
dare to be. I say this, however, not pejoratively but admiringly.
You cannot read Whitman without laughing at him—he is simply
outrageous; but then Whitman reminds the reader ever and again

and quite correctly that he issued the invitation to laughter and that he was himself the first to laugh. He was no more outrageous than Emily Dickinson, however, when the fit was upon her as it surely was in poem #577. Walt Whitman, in his large alimentiveness, might imagine feeding on his readers and imagine them feeding on him, and he might croon hymns to lovely, soothing, cool-enfolding, undulating death, but he never, like Dickinson, engaged in blissful fantasies of necrophilia. Commentators tend to shy away from poem #577 or, if they treat the poem at all, they discover implausible referents for the "it" of the first line— "If I may have it, when it's dead"—but I think it is only one mark among many of Dickinson's strangeness that, if she is going to write a poem about her love surviving the beloved's death, she should treat the subject in the most literal way and imagine herself fondling "it"—her lover's corpse—and finding in the act a "Bliss I cannot weigh."

> If I may have it, when it's dead,
> I'll be contented—so—
> If just as soon as Breath is out
> It shall belong to me—
>
> Until they lock it in the Grave,
> 'Tis Bliss I cannot weigh—
> For tho' they lock Thee in the Grave,
> Myself—can own the key—
>
> Think of it Lover! I and Thee
> Permitted—face to face to be—
> After a Life—a Death—We'll say—
> For Death was That—
> And this—is Thee—
>
> I'll tell Thee All—how Bald it grew—
> How Midnight felt, at first—to me—

How all the Clocks stopped in the World —
And Sunshine pinched me — 'Twas so cold —

Then how the Grief got sleepy — some —
As if my Soul were deaf and dumb —
Just making signs — across — to Thee —
That this way — thou could'st notice me —

I'll tell you how I tried to keep
A smile, to show you, when this Deep
All waded — We look back for Play,
At those Old Times — in Calvary.

Forgive me, if the Grave come slow —
For Coveting to look at Thee —
Forgive me, if to stroke thy frost
Outvisions Paradise!

"Think of it Lover!" — just think of it! The central premise of this poem, that if the speaker cannot have the beloved when alive she will be more than happy to make do with his corpse when dead — "to stroke thy frost / Outvisions Paradise!" — is so bizarre that it quite throws into the shade the odd but altogether characteristic Dickinsonian gesture in the third stanza of reversing life and death: "After a Life — a Death — We'll say — / For Death was That — / And this — is Thee —" Although Dickinson has left so much out here that it is difficult to recover the meaning, this seems to suggest (and this would be thoroughly Dickinsonian) that that so-called Life before Death was real Death, and this, which is the lover's corpse, is, for the speaker, full of Life now after Death.

The necrophilia of poem #577 is an unusual twist even for Dickinson, a heightening of an already heightened strangeness, but in its linguistic compression and its darting, quicksilver, elliptical ungraspableness it is not unlike the rest of her seventeen-hundred-plus poems. And the same holds true for Hopkins and Whitman as well. Different as they were from one another in so

many ways, they were alike in this: that they were different in
absolutely consistent and continuous ways. Hopkins was Hopkins,
Dickinson Dickinson, and Whitman Whitman from beginning
to end, and their bodies of work—poems, letters, and any other
prose—are all of a piece, all stamped with their unique, individual
seal and style. One might think of their bodies of work as reflections or expressions of their literal, physical bodies, all of them
strange to think of: the body of Emily Dickinson, the body of
Walt Whitman, the body of Gerard Hopkins, each peculiar, each
eerie, moving in a world filled with normal, bland bodies of sameness. It is a peculiarity about making strange that it has to do with
defamiliarizing the world we live in so that we see anew, as it were
with quickened eyes; and yet making strange defamiliarizes in
such a distinctive manner that we find ourselves as readers going
beyond familiarity to identify with the worlds newly imagined by
Dickinson, Hopkins, Whitman.

Hopkins could have been speaking for all three of them and
for their readers when he wrote of individual distinctiveness as
follows:

And this is much more true when we consider the mind;
when I consider my selfbeing, my consciousness and feeling of myself, that taste of myself, of *I* and *me* above and in
all things, which is more distinctive than the taste of ale or
alum, more distinctive than the smell of walnutleaf or cam-
phor, and is incommunicable by any means to another man
(as when I was a child I used to ask myself: What must it
be to be someone else?). Nothing else in nature comes near
this unspeakable stress of pitch, distinctiveness, and selving,
this selfbeing of my own. Nothing explains it or resembles
it, except so far as this, that other men to themselves have
the same feeling. But this only multiplies the phenomena to
be explained so far as the cases are like and do resemble. But
to me there is no resemblance: searching nature I taste *self*

but at one tankard, that of my own being. The development, refinement, condensation of nothing shews any sign of being able to match this to me or give me another taste of it, a taste even resembling it (*Sermons and Devotional Writings*, p 123).

Hopkins's phrasing suggests that for him, and any reader must feel that the same is true for Dickinson and Whitman as well, every individual who really is individual is almost like a separate species, existing in her/his own uniqueness. Hopkins's way of expressing himself here is very nearly related to the notion of *haecceitas* — the *thisness* of individual beings — that Hopkins found so congenial in Duns Scotus. It is the *haecceitas* of their conjoint being and making — for in the end, the being and the making are not really separable — that permits us to speak of poems as Hopkinsian, Dickinsonian, Whitmanian and know what we mean; and yet, besides this heightened distinctiveness there must be elements of similarity, there must be that that the three poets have in common that allows us to recognize their poems not only as theirs but also as poems — poems of depth and of importance to us in our attempt to understand our own experience. There may be other things they have in common, but I have suggested that a heightened rhythmization of language, a heightened figurativity of language, and a distinctive strangeness about the vision and the technical means used to express it should always indicate to us that it is a poet of consequence that we are reading.

Notes

1. SPRUNG RHYTHM, COMMON METER, AND THE BARBARIC YAWP

1. Actually we know what Arnold would have said of Whitman. Responding to a complimentary copy of *The Good Gray Poet*, a polemical pamphlet in favor of *Leaves of Grass*, Arnold wrote to its author, William O'Connor: "As to the general question of Mr. Walt Whitman's poetical achievement, I add that while you think it is his highest merit that he is so unlike anyone else, to me this seems to be his demerit; no one can afford in literature to trade merely on his own bottom and to take no account of what other ages and nations have acquired: a great original literature America will never get in this way" (Justin Kaplan, *Walt Whitman: A Life* [New York: Simon & Schuster, 1980], pp. 320–21).

2. It is interesting to consider what—had they read it—Whitman and Dickinson would have thought of one another's poetry. Whitman, of course, was entirely unaware of Dickinson; Dickinson, on the other hand, responded to a query from T. W. Higginson thus: "You speak of Walt Whitman—I never read his Book—but was told that he was disgraceful—" (*The Letters of Emily Dickinson*, #261). Hopkins, in a similar vein, referred to Whitman as "a very great scoundrel" (*The Letters of Gerard Manley Hopkins to Robert Bridges*, p. 155), but he seems not to have known much more of Whitman's poetry than Dickinson knew.

3. This is the beginning of Dickinson's poem #448:

> This was a Poet—It is That
> Distills amazing sense
> From ordinary Meanings—
> And Attar so immense
> From the familiar species
> That perished by the Door—

It is appropriate here to quote Dickinson on what would prove to her that a piece of writing might merit the high name of poetry: "If I read a book [and] it makes my whole body so cold no fire ever can warm me I know *that* is poetry. If I feel physically as if the top of my head were taken off, I know *that* is poetry. These are the only way I know it. Is there any other way" (from Higginson's description of Emily Dickinson's conversation, *The Letters of Emily Dickinson*, #342a).

4. Paul Valéry, *The Art of Poetry*, tr. Denise Folliot, vol. 7 in *The Collected Works of Paul Valéry*, ed. Jackson Mathews (New York: Bollingen Foundation/Pantheon Books, 1958), pp. 61–62.

5. Seamus Heaney, *Preoccupations: Selected Prose 1968–1978* (London: Faber & Faber, 1980), p. 65.

6. T. S. Eliot, "The Music of Poetry," in *On Poetry and Poets* (New York: Farrar, Straus, 1957), p. 32.

7. Gertrude Stein, *Everybody's Autobiography* (New York: Random House, 1937), pp. 223–24.

8. Henry James, "Walt Whitman," in *Henry James: Essays on Literature, American Writers, English Writers* (New York: Library of America, 1984), p. 631.

9. In 1898 James reviewed Whitman's letters to Peter Doyle with high praise, saying, among other things, that in those letters as in *Leaves of Grass*, Whitman is "an upright figure, a *successful* original" (James, "Walt Whitman," p. 662). In later years, James was profoundly embarrassed about his review of *Drum Taps*. He described it in a letter to Manton Marble of 1903 as "the little atrocity I . . . perpetrated (on W.W.) in the gross impudence of youth." Nothing, James went on, "would induce me to reveal the whereabouts of my disgrace, which I only recollect as deep and damning. . . . I haven't seen the accursed thing for more than thirty years, and . . . if it were to cross my path nothing would induce me to look at it. I am so far from 'keeping' the abominations of my early innocence that I destroy them wherever I spy them" (James, *Selected Letters*, ed. Leon Edel [Cambridge, Mass.: Harvard University Press, 1987], p. 348). In these same years, according to Edith Wharton's description, James read Whitman with the deepest feeling himself and with the profoundest effect on his audience. After describing James's reading of poetry in general ("He chanted it, and he was not afraid to chant it, as many good

readers are, who, though they instinctively feel that the genius of the English poetical idiom requires it to be spoken *as poetry*, are yet afraid of yielding to their instinct because the present-day fashion is to chatter high verse as though it were colloquial prose. James, on the contrary, far from shirking the rhythmic emphasis, gave it full expression.") Wharton continues with an evocation of James reading Whitman: "Another day some one spoke of Whitman, and it was a joy to me to discover that James thought him, as I did, the greatest of American poets. 'Leaves of Grass' was put into his hands, and all that evening we sat rapt while he wandered from 'The Song of Myself' to 'When lilacs last in the door-yard bloomed' (when he read 'Lovely and soothing Death' his voice filled the hushed room like an organ adagio), and thence let himself be lured on to the mysterious music of 'Out of the Cradle,' reading, or rather crooning it in a mood of subdued ecstasy till the fivefold invocation to Death tolled out like the knocks in the opening bars of the Fifth Symphony." For all his feeling for Whitman's rhythmic splendors, however, James all the same retained his youthful skepticism about the value of Whitman's displays of foreign-language learning, as we see in the conclusion to Edith Wharton's description: "James's admiration of Whitman, his immediate response to that mighty appeal, was a new proof of the way in which, above a certain level, the most divergent intelligences walk together like gods. We talked long that night of 'Leaves of Grass,' tossing back and forth to each other treasure after treasure; but finally James, in one of his sudden humorous drops from the heights, flung up his hands and cried out with the old stammer and twinkle: 'Oh, yes, a great genius; undoubtedly a very great genius! Only one cannot help deploring his too-extensive acquaintance with the foreign languages.'" (Edith Wharton, *A Backward Glance* [New York: Charles Scribner's Sons, 1964], pp. 185–86.)

10. Eliot, "Reflections on *Vers Libre*," in *To Criticize the Critic* (London: Faber & Faber, 1965), pp. 187–88.

11. Donald Gallup, "Mr. Eliot at the Churchill Club," *Southern Review* 21 (1985): 969–73.

12. *In Re Walt Whitman*, ed. Horace L. Traubel, Richard Maurice Bucke, and Thomas B. Harned (Philadelphia: David McKay, 1893), p. 13.

13. Autrey Nell Wiley, "Reiterative Devices in *Leaves of Grass*," *American Literature* 1 (May 1929), p. 161.

14. Isaac Watts, *The Psalms of David, imitated in the Language of the New Testament and Applied to the Christian State and Worship. Together with Hymns and Spiritual Songs in Three Books* (Northampton: William Butler, 1799). "When I can read my title clear" is designated b65 — that is, it is hymn 65 in book 2.

15. This poem is not in Common Meter but in Nines and Eights, which are, nevertheless, all tetrameter lines. This meter, while relatively infrequent in hymnals, is not unknown there.

16. Watts, *The Psalms of David*, c14.

17. *Ibid.*, a19.

18. *The Correspondence of Gerard Manley Hopkins and Richard Watson Dixon*, ed. Claude Colleer Abbott (London: Oxford University Press, 1935), p. 14.

19. *The Journals and Papers of Gerard Manley Hopkins*, ed. Humphry House and Graham Storey (London: Oxford University Press, 1959), p. 271.

20. "Author's Preface on Rhythm," in *The Poetical Works of Gerard Manley Hopkins*, ed. Norman H. MacKenzie (Oxford: Clarendon Press, 1990), p. 116.

21. Consider Hopkins's description of the aftereffects of a nightmare when he had lost this inner rhythm and harmony of physical being: "I had lost all muscular stress elsewhere but not sensitive, feeling where each limb lay and thinking that I could recover myself if I could move a finger, I said, and then the arm and so the whole body. The feeling is terrible: the body no longer swayed as a piece by the nervous and muscular instress seems to fall in and hang like a dead weight on the chest. I cried on the holy name and by degrees recovered myself as I thought to do. It made me think that this was how the souls in hell would be imprisoned in their bodies as in prisons" (*Journals*, p. 238).

22. *The Letters of Gerard Manley Hopkins to Robert Bridges*, ed. Abbott (London: Oxford University Press, 1935), p. 44.

23. *Further Letters of Gerard Manley Hopkins*, 2d edn., ed. Abbott (London: Oxford University Press, 1956), p. 138.

2. TROPES OF PRESENCE, TROPES OF ABSENCE

1. Howard Nemerov, "On Metaphor," in *New and Selected Essays* (Carbondale & Edwardsville: University of Southern Illinois Press, 1985), p. 114.

2. René Wellek and Austin Warren, *Theory of Literature* (New York: Harcourt, Brace, 1956), p. 183.

3. I do not include Kenneth Burke's fourth "master trope" of irony because, while it might contribute a great deal to understanding Dickinson, I think it would not be particularly helpful in discussing Whitman or Hopkins. Metonymy and metaphor, on the other hand, tell us something about the practices of all three poets—if only, at times, by way of contrast.

4. On the loss and absence that become a virtual presence in Dickinson's poetry, see #1551, which concludes, however, that we would do better to maintain belief in the illusions of religion even though we know they are no more than illusions:

> Those—dying then,
> Knew where they went—
> They went to God's Right Hand—
> That Hand is amputated now
> And God cannot be found—
>
> The abdication of Belief
> Makes the Behavior small—
> Better an ignis fatuus
> Than no illume at all—

5. The phrase "absent presence" I have borrowed from an extremely interesting book by Ronald Fraser, *In Search of a Past*, where, however, it is used in a context quite different from my own.

6. Passages taken passim from the 1855 preface to *Leaves of Grass*, pp. 5–26 in *Walt Whitman: Poetry and Prose*.

7. Kenneth Burke, *A Grammar of Motives* (New York: Prentice-Hall, 1945), p. 508.

8. That it was poems like this one that drew Anne Gilchrist on we can see in a letter to Whitman like the following: "Besides, it is not true thou

hast not sought or loved me. For when I read the divine poems I feel all
folded round in thy love; I feel often as if thou wast pleading so passion-
ately for the love of the woman that can understand thee—that I know
not how to bear the yearning answering tenderness that fills my breast"
(*The Letters of Anne Gilchrist and Walt Whitman*, p. 66).

9. Emily Dickinson was not always so far removed from Walt Whitman—or perhaps one should say from Anne Gilchrist—as one tends to
think. Consider poem #249:

> Wild Nights—Wild Nights!
> Were I with thee
> Wild Nights should be
> Our luxury!
>
> Futile—the Winds—
> To a Heart in port—
> Done with the Compass—
> Done with the Chart!
>
> Rowing in Eden—
> Ah, the Sea!
> Might I but moor—Tonight—
> In Thee!

10. This combination of the metonymic and metaphoric one finds
again, though not so intensely sustained, in a poem like "The Blessed
Virgin compared to the Air we Breathe," which begins, "Wild air, world-
mothering air, / Nestling me everywhere," and that later has the lines,
"I say that we are wound / With mercy round and round / As if with
air. . . ." The working of metonymy, with its implications of presentness
and contiguity, is particularly prominent in some of Hopkins's journal
entries—the following for example: "July 22—Very hot, though the wind,
which was south, dappled very sweetly on one's face and when I came out
I seemed to put it on like a gown as a man puts on the shadow he walks
into and hoods or hats himself with the shelter of a roof, a penthouse,
or a copse of trees, I mean it rippled and fluttered like light linen, one
could feel the folds and braids of it—and indeed a floating flag is like

wind visible and what weeds are in a current; it gives it thew and fires it and bloods it in" (*Journals*, p. 233).

11. Or if not mystical then at least Platonic: Hopkins seems to have believed that there was a Sonnet Form laid away in heaven which real sonnets were more or less successful in imitating. Thus he reproved Richard Watson Dixon for sonnets that "are very, I must say unpardonably, licentious in form." Hopkins went on to describe the form of the true sonnet:

"Now it seems to me that this division [into the two parts 8 + 6] is the real characteristic of the sonnet and that what is not so marked off and moreover has not the octet again divided into quatrains is not to be called a sonnet at all. For in the cipher 14 is no mystery and if one does not know nor avail oneself of the opportunities which it affords it is a pedantic encumbrance and not an advantage. The equation of the best sonnet is

$$(4 + 4) + (3 + 3) = 2.4 + 2.3 = 2(4 + 3) = 2.7 = 14.$$

This means several things — (A) that the sonnet is one of the works of art of which the equation or construction is unsymmetrical in the shape $x + y = a$, where x and y are unequal in some simple ratio, as $2:1$, $3:2$, $4:3$. . . . (B) It is divided symmetrically too in multiples of two, as all effects taking place in time tend to be. . . . (C) It pairs off even or symmetrical members with symmetrical (the quatrains) and uneven or unsymmetrical with uneven (the tercets). And even the rhymes, did time allow, I could shew are founded on a principle of nature and cannot be altered without loss of effect" (*Correspondence of GMH and RWD*, pp. 71–72).

Hopkins was very strict in his own observance of these principles of the sonnet and was one of the great sonnet writers in the English tradition.

12. In the letter to Bridges in which he defends himself against the charge of influence from Whitman, Hopkins describes the extent of his knowledge of Whitman: "I have read of Whitman's (1) 'Pete' [i.e., "Come up from the fields father"] in the library at Bedford Square (and perhaps something else; if so I forget), which you pointed out; (2) two pieces in the *Athenaeum* or *Academy*, one on the Man-of-War Bird, the other beginning 'Spirit that formed this scene'; (3) short extracts in a review by

Saintsbury in the *Academy*; this is all I remember. I cannot have read more than half a dozen pieces at most." Hopkins goes on to analyze Whitman's rhythm at some length and quotes what he calls "a fragment of a line I remember: 'or a handkerchief designedly dropped'" (*Letters to RB*, pp. 154–55). This was from one of the extracts in Saintsbury's review that appeared in October 1874. Since Hopkins was writing to Bridges in October 1882 — eight years after the review appeared — it is less surprising that he slightly misquotes the line than that he remembered it as accurately as he did. One must wonder how many other lines and fragments of lines of Whitman remained in Hopkins's mind from the sparse reading he had done in *Leaves of Grass*.

13. When Whitman says he sees God in his own face in the glass I am reminded of a very striking passage in Newman's *Apologia pro vita sua*: "Starting then with the being of a God, (which, as I have said, is as certain to me as the certainty of my own existence . . .) I look out of myself into the world of men, and there I see a sight which fills me with unspeakable distress. The world seems simply to give the lie to that great truth, of which my whole being is so full; and the effect upon me is, in consequence, as a matter of necessity, as confusing as if it denied that I am in existence myself. If I looked into a mirror, and did not see my face, I should have the sort of feeling which actually comes upon me, when I look into this living busy world, and see no reflection of its Creator" (*Apologia pro vita sua* [New York: Modern Library, 1950], pp. 239–40). This was not Whitman's ordinary experience — when he looked into the mirror he saw not only his own but God's reflection — but it does seem to me eerily accurate for Dickinson often and Hopkins sometimes: when they looked into the mirror they saw neither their own nor God's reflection.

14. See Emily Dickinson's poem #441, which begins "This is my letter to the World / That never wrote to Me. . . ."

15. In a letter of April 1884 to Bridges, Hopkins suddenly breaks into capital letters to ask "AND WHAT DOES ANYTHING AT ALL MATTER?" One might be inclined to think this merely another instance of Hopkins's unusual epistolary manner except that it comes in the context of letters that exhibit signs of profound depression — for example, this note added to a letter to Bridges two weeks later: "I am, I believe, recovering from a deep

fit of nervous prostration (I suppose I ought to call it): I did not know but I was dying" (*Letters to RB*, pp. 192–93).

3. MAKING STRANGE

1. Gay Wilson Allen, *The Solitary Singer: A Critical Biography of Walt Whitman* (New York: Macmillan, 1955), p. 173.

2. See the second of Whitman's poems titled "To You": "Old or young, male or female, rude, low, rejected by the rest, whatever you are promulges itself." To "promulge"—wonderful Whitmanian word—is surely the same as to go "its self; *myself* it speaks and spells."

3. I think an interesting case could be made for saying that Whitman, Dickinson, and Hopkins were, in the first instance, all self-published. Critics dispute whether Dickinson and Hopkins ever desired publication. I think they both did, but on their own terms. Dickinson was very careful in gathering fair copies of her poems together into fascicles, as it were separate booklets of poems, that could represent something like private publication. And Hopkins took equal care to have his poems collected in a single book—and in what he wanted to be their final form. Writing early on to Bridges, Hopkins declared, "When I say that I do not mean to publish I speak the truth." But he went on to say, "All therefore that I think of doing is to keep my verses together in one place—at present I have not even correct copies—, that, if anyone shd. like, they might be published after my death" (*Letters to RB*, p. 66). Bridges, as Hopkins knew, was keeping a manuscript book of his poems as he sent them to Bridges, and later Hopkins asked Bridges to copy out the manuscript book and send him the copy so that he might make corrections in the poems already in it and add to the collection new poems as they were produced. Hopkins kept this collection in the state he would have wished for publication except for the "sonnets of desolation," fragments, and certain other late poems that were recovered from his papers after his death.

4. Norman H. MacKenzie, *A Reader's Guide to Gerard Manley Hopkins* (Ithaca: Cornell University Press, 1981), p. 86.

5. Whitman's self-confidence scarcely needs noting; on the other hand, it is interesting to see how much alike Dickinson and Hopkins, neither of whom actively or wholeheartedly sought publication, were in

their self-assurance. Here is Hopkins writing to Robert Bridges, in a very characteristic vein, about "The Wreck of the Deutschland": "I cannot think of altering anything. Why shd. I? I do not write for the public. You are my public and I hope to convert you. You say you wd. not for any money read my poem again. Nevertheless I beg you will. Besides money, you know, there is love. If it is obscure do not bother yourself with the meaning but pay attention to the best and most intelligible stanzas, as the two last of each part and the narrative of the wreck. If you had done this you wd. have liked it better and sent me some serviceable criticisms, but now your criticism is of no use, being only a protest memorialising me against my whole policy and proceedings" (*Letters to RB*, pp. 46–47). Dickinson would never write to Higginson "I cannot think of altering anything," but this is due merely to a different temperament and different tactics, not to any self-doubt on her part; the different language in which she would have expressed herself aside, Dickinson, I believe, would have subscribed to everything in Hopkins's letter. And I do not think that we can be at all sure that for all her posing as "your gnome" and "your scholar" Dickinson did not include Higginson—privately, in her own feelings—among those "Men" beyond whose estimate she claims to have risen in poem #798.

6. Catherine Phillips, *Gerard Manley Hopkins* (Oxford & New York: Oxford University Press, 1986), p. 381. Norman H. MacKenzie has this note on the word "heft" in the now standard edition of Hopkins's poetry: "Trench, *Eng. Past and Present* (1881), 204, listed 'heft' among 'Good Words Extinct'" (*The Poetical Works of Gerard Manley Hopkins*, p. 477). It is interesting and very much to the point that all three of our poets should have been using this "Good Word" at virtually the same moment that Trench observed it to be "Extinct."

7. This is the 1881 version of "A Song for Occupations"; the version that appeared in the 1855 *Leaves of Grass* is quite different and lacks both the "strange and hard paradox" I have cited and the conclusion that in these mundane matters are to be found "poems for you and me."

8. Both of these poems bear quoting at some length to show how far Whitman went in his attempt to expand the limits of poetry in accepting "unpoetic" language. "The child of the glutton or the venerealee" is in-

cluded in the following list of those who, in "The Sleepers," are said to
be "all beautiful":

The homeward bound and the outward bound,
The beautiful lost swimmer, the ennuyé, the onanist, the female that
loves unrequited, the money-maker . . . ,
The laugher and weeper, the dancer, the midnight widow, the
red squaw,
The consumptive, the erysipalite, the idiot, he that is wrong'd. . . .

And here is "A Hand-Mirror" in its entirety:

Hold it up sternly—see this it sends back, (who is it? is it you?)
Outside fair costume, within ashes and filth,
No more a flashing eye, no more a sonorous voice or springy step,
Now some slave's eye, voice, hands, step,
A drunkard's breath, unwholesome eater's face, venerealee's flesh,
Lungs rotting away piecemeal, stomach sour and cankerous,
Joints rheumatic, bowels clogged with abomination,
Blood circulating dark and poisonous streams,
Words babble, hearing and touch callous,
No brain, no heart left, no magnetism of sex;
Such from one look in this looking-glass ere you go hence,
Such a result so soon—and from such a beginning!

9. From the 1855 preface: "The English language befriends the grand
American expression . . . it is brawny enough and limber and full enough.
On the tough stock of a race who through all change of circumstances
was never without the idea of political liberty, which is the animus of all
liberty, it has attracted the terms of daintier and gayer and subtler and
more elegant tongues. It is the powerful language of resistance . . . it is the
dialect of common sense. It is the speech of the proud and melancholy
races and of all who aspire. It is the chosen tongue to express growth faith
self-esteem freedom justice equality friendliness amplitude prudence de-
cision and courage. It is the medium that shall well nigh express the
inexpressible" (*Walt Whitman: Poetry and Prose*, p. 25; ellipsis points in
the original).

10. Dickinson's letter echoes the imagery of poem #754, "My Life

had stood—a Loaded Gun—"; its terms of barely contained explosive force also no doubt account for Higginson's reaction upon first meeting Dickinson after some eight years of correspondence (as reported by Higginson to his wife): "I never was with any one who drained my nerve power so much. Without touching her, she drew from me. I am glad not to live near her" (*Letters,* #342b).

Bibliography

I. TEXTS OF EMILY DICKINSON, GERARD MANLEY HOPKINS, WALT WHITMAN

The Poems of Emily Dickinson, 3 vols. Ed. Thomas H. Johnson. Cambridge, Mass.: Harvard University Press, 1955.

The Letters of Emily Dickinson, 3 vols. Ed. Thomas H. Johnson. Cambridge, Mass.: Harvard University Press, 1958.

The Poetical Works of Gerard Manley Hopkins. Ed. Norman H. MacKenzie. Oxford: Clarendon Press, 1990.

Gerard Manley Hopkins, Oxford Authors Series. Ed. Catherine Phillips. Oxford: Oxford University Press, 1986.

The Journals and Papers of Gerard Manley Hopkins. Ed. Humphry House and Graham Storey. Oxford: Oxford University Press, 1959.

The Sermons and Devotional Writings of Gerard Manley Hopkins. Ed. Christopher Devlin. Oxford: Oxford University Press, 1959.

The Letters of Gerard Manley Hopkins to Robert Bridges. Ed. Claude Colleer Abbott. Oxford: Oxford University Press, 1955.

The Correspondence of Gerard Manley Hopkins and Richard Watson Dixon. Ed. Abbott. Oxford: Oxford University Press, 1955.

Further Letters of Gerard Manley Hopkins, 2d edn. Ed. Abbott. Oxford: Oxford University Press, 1956.

Walt Whitman: Poetry and Prose. Ed. Justin Kaplan. New York: Library of America, 1982.

The Collected Writings of Walt Whitman: The Correspondence, 5 vols. Ed. Edwin Haviland Miller. New York: New York University Press, 1961–69.

The Letters of Anne Gilchrist and Walt Whitman. Ed. Thomas B. Harned. Garden City, N.Y.: Doubleday, Page, 1918.

In Re Walt Whitman. Ed. Horace L. Traubel, Richard Maurice Bucke, and Thomas B. Harned. Philadelphia: David McKay, 1893.

II. OTHER WORKS CITED

Allen, Gay Wilson. *The Solitary Singer: A Critical Biography of Walt Whitman*. New York: Macmillan, 1955.

Berryman, John. *The Freedom of the Poet*. New York: Farrar, Straus & Giroux, 1976.

Burke, Kenneth. *A Grammar of Motives*. New York: Prentice-Hall, 1945.

Eliot, T. S. *On Poetry and Poets*. New York: Farrar, Straus, 1961.

——. *To Criticize the Critic and Other Writings*. London: Faber & Faber, 1965.

England, Martha Winburn. *Hymns Unbidden: Donne, Herbert, Blake, Emily Dickinson, and the Hymnographers*. New York: New York Public Library, 1966.

Fraser, Ronald. *In Search of a Past: The Manor House, Amnersfield 1933–1945*. London: Verso, 1984.

Heaney, Seamus. *Preoccupations: Selected Prose 1968–1978*. London: Faber & Faber, 1980.

James, Henry. *Literary Criticism: Essays on Literature, American Writers, English Writers*. Ed. Leon Edel. New York: Library of America, 1984.

——. *Selected Letters*. Ed. Leon Edel. Cambridge, Mass.: Harvard University Press, 1987.

Johnson, Thomas H. *Emily Dickinson: An Interpretive Biography*. Cambridge, Mass.: Harvard University Press, 1955.

MacKenzie, Norman H. *A Reader's Guide to Gerard Manley Hopkins*. Ithaca: Cornell University Press, 1981.

Nemerov, Howard. *New and Selected Essays*. Carbondale & Edwardsville: Southern Illinois University Press, 1985.

Newman, John Henry. *Apologia pro vita sua*. New York: Modern Library, 1950.

Ricoeur, Paul. *The Rule of Metaphor: Multi-disciplinary Studies of the Creation of Meaning in Language*. Tr. Robert Czerny with Kathleen McLaughlin and John Costello, SJ. Toronto: University of Toronto Press, 1977.

Stein, Gertrude. *Everybody's Autobiography*. New York: Random House, 1937.

Valéry, Paul. *The Art of Poetry*. Tr. Denise Folliot. Vol. 7 of *The Collected Works of Paul Valéry*.Ed. Jackson Mathews. New York: Bollingen Foundation/Pantheon Books, 1958.

Watts, Isaac. *The Psalms of David, Imitated in the Language of the New Testament and Applied to the Christian State and Worship. Together with Hymns and Spiritual Songs in Three Books*. Northampton: William Butler, 1799.

Wellek, René, and Austin Warren. *Theory of Literature*. New York: Harcourt, Brace, 1956.

Wharton, Edith. *A Backward Glance*. New York: Appleton-Century, 1934. Reprint. New York: Scribners, 1964.

Wiley, Autrey Nell. "Reiterative Devices in *Leaves of Grass*." *American Literature* 1 (1929), pp. 161–70.

Index

Duns Scotus, John, 137

Einstein, Albert, 97
Eliot, T. S., 38, 63, 98, 140 (n. 6),
141 (n. 10); "The Music of
Poetry," 8, 9; "Walt Whitman
and Modern Poetry," 19–20;
"The Waste Land," 62; "The
Lovesong of J. Alfred
Prufrock," 70
Everybody's Autobiography, 14–16,
140 (n. 7)

Forster, E. M., 18
"Four Master Tropes," 68
Fraser, Ronald, 143 (n. 5)
Freedom of the Poet, The, 63

Gallup, Donald, 19–20, 141 (n. 11)
Gilchrist, Anne: correspondence
with Walt Whitman, 70–71,
143–44 (n. 8)
Ginsberg, Allen, 2

Hampson, Alfred Leete, 30
Hazlitt, William, 6–7, 21, 38
Heaney, Seamus, 6–8, 21, 38, 140
(n. 5)
Herbert, George, 84
Higginson, T. W.: correspondence with Emily Dickinson,
56, 62, 92, 99, 100, 101, 111–12,
113, 130–31, 139 (n. 2), 140
(n. 3), 148 (n. 5), 150 (n. 10)
Hopkins, Gerard Manley:
works— "As kingfishers catch
fire," 38–39, 80, 95, 96–97;
"Binsey Poplars," 13; "The
Blessed Virgin Compared to

the Air we Breathe," 144–45
(n. 10); "The Caged Skylark,"
39; "Duns Scotus's Oxford,"
105; "Epithalamion," 78–80, 83;
"God's Grandeur," 38, 80, 81,
87, 88, 102; "Harry Ploughman," 122, 124, 128; "Henry
Purcell," 96–97; "Hurrahing in
Harvest," 39, 89; "In the Valley
of the Elwy," 39; "Inversnaid,"
89, 104–5; "I wake and feel the
fell of dark, not day," 85–86;
Journals and Papers, 83, 86–87,
92, 105, 106, 142 (nn. 19, 20, 22);
"Justus quidem tu es, Domine,"
89–90; "The Lantern out of
Doors," 39; "The Leaden Echo
and the Golden Echo," 42, 128;
"Morning, Midday, and
Evening Sacrifice," 105; "No
worst," 87, 130, 132; "On the
Portrait of Two Beautiful
Young People," 114; "Pied
Beauty," 39, 89, 103–4, 105–6,
107; "The Sea and the Skylark,"
39; *Sermons and Devotional
Writings*, 81, 84, 136–37; "Spelt
from Sibyl's Leaves," 87–88, 89,
105, 107; "Spring," 39, 80, 89;
"The Starlight Night," 38;
"That Nature is a Hericlitean
Fire and of the comfort of the
Resurrection," 96, 101; "Tom's
Garland," 122, 125; "To R. B.,"
89–91; "To What Serves
Mortal Beauty?," 78, 128; "The
Windhover," 39, 81–85, 87, 89,
105; "The Wreck of the